An Unforgettable
AFTER-GRAD

To Justin + Michele
With thanks for your tremendous support + friendship
Linda ♡

An Unforgettable
AFTER-GRAD

Your guide to creating
and operating a successful
all-night safe, dry, grad event

LINDA HUNTER

151 Howe Street, Victoria BC Canada V8V 4K5

Copyright © 2010, Linda Hunter
All rights reserved

Without limiting the rights under copyright reserved above, no part of this publication may be reproduced, stored in or introduced into a retrieval system, or transmitted, in any form or by any means (electronic, mechanical, photocopying, recording or otherwise), without the prior written permission of both the copyright owner and the publisher of this book.

DISCLAIMER

The author of this book does not dispense legal or medical advice or guarantee an alcohol-free, drug-free, or problem-free After-Grad. The intent of the author is only to offer information of a general nature to assist in the planning of a safe, dry, all-night After-Grad event. In the event you use any of the information in this book, the author and the publisher disclaim all responsibility for any liability, loss, or risk, personal or otherwise, which is incurred as a consequence directly or indirectly, of the use of application of any of the contents of this book.

For rights information and bulk orders, please contact:
info@agiopublishing.com or go to
www.agiopublishing.com

An Unforgettable AFTER-GRAD
ISBN 978-1-897435-46-5 (trade paperback)

Author's website
www.safegradevent.com

Printed on acid-free paper. Agio Publishing House is a socially responsible company, measuring success on a triple-bottom-line basis.

10 9 8 7 6 5 4 3 2 1

For my family

who make every adventure worthwhile

and who continue to teach me the meaning of 'fearless'

ACKNOWLEDGEMENTS

I am deeply grateful to so many individuals for providing assistance and support during my five years producing After-Grad events and the writing of this book. While there are too many to mention I am in particular thankful to the Parkland Secondary School community for their unwavering enthusiasm and support of my efforts and to Sharon Woods who first introduced me to the idea of a safe, dry, all-night event for our own graduating children and whose unconditional friendship and belief in me, along with countless volunteer hours, was instrumental in the success of our After-Grads.

TABLE OF CONTENTS

Why Dry?
    An Introduction To The Dry After-Grad Concept   1

How To Use This Book   5

Making It Unforgettable!   9

Building the Excitement   13

SEPTEMBER   17
    Chair   19

OCTOBER   23
    Chair   25
    Communications & Publicity   31

NOVEMBER   33
    Chair   35
    Communications & Publicity   40
    Finance   46
    Volunteer   50
    Transportation, Operations & Safety   51
    Decorating, Food & Beverage   58
    Entertainment, Games & Contests   63
    Fundraising & Prizes   67

DECEMBER ... 73

JANUARY ... 75
    Communications & Publicity ... 77
    Volunteer ... 77

FEBRUARY ... 79
    Chair ... 81
    Communications & Publicity ... 84
    Fundraising & Prizes ... 85

MARCH ... 87
    Chair ... 89
    Communications & Publicity ... 90
    Finance ... 90
    Volunteer ... 91
    Transportation, Operations & Safety ... 93
    Decorating, Food & Beverage ... 94
    Entertainment, Games & Contests ... 95
    Fundraising & Prizes ... 96

APRIL ... 99
    Chair ... 101
    Communications & Publicity ... 101
    Volunteer ... 102
    Transportation, Operations & Safety ... 102
    Decorating, Food & Beverage ... 103
    Entertainment, Games & Contests ... 106

MAY ... 109
    Communications & Publicity ... 111
    Volunteer ... 113
    Transportation, Operations & Safety ... 114
    Decorating, Food & Beverage ... 117
    Entertainment, Games, & Contests ... 121
    Fundraising & Prizes ... 124

JUNE	129
PRE EVENT	131
Chair	131
Communications & Publicity	132
Finance	132
Volunteers	133
Transportation, Operations & Safety	134
Decorating, Food & Beverage	135
Entertainment, Games, Contests	136
Fundraising & Prizes	136
THE AFTER-GRAD EVENT	138
POST EVENT	142
AG Committee Debrief Meeting	142
ACTION ITEM CALENDARS	
September	18
October	24
November	34
December	74
January	76
February	80
March	88
April	100
May	110
June	130
APPENDIX – FORMS	145
Volunteer Form – September	146
Venue Questions – October	147–148
Event Flow – November	149
Survey – November	150
Survey Report – November	151
Quote Sheet – November	152
Supplier Contact List – November	153
Event Budget – November	154–156
Supplier Questions – November	157
Food Provider Questions – November	158

Performer Questions – November	159
Prize Solicitation Letter – November	160
Tuition Solicitation Letter – November	161
Grad Attendance Agreement – February	162–163
Guest Attendance Agreement – February	164–165
Event Schedule – March	166–171
Volunteer Grid – March	172–174
Installation Schedule – March	175
Floor Plan – April	176
Master Attendance List – May	177
Master Guest List – May	178
Supplier Agreement – May	179
Food & Beverage Order – May	180
Performer Agreement – May	181
Bus Escort Script – June	182
Budget Analysis – June	183
Author Bio	185

Why Dry?

An introduction to the dry After-Grad concept

For grade twelve students and their families, high school graduation – a milestone recognizing over a decade of school achievements – is a time of celebration filled with social events. This special grad year often culminates in a graduation ceremony, sometimes followed by a school-sponsored celebration, and then, for many, the all-important "all-night grad party."

Unfortunately, many of these all night parties have come to represent a rite of passage and include underage drinking, drugs, unsafe sex and other high risk behaviours, and in some cases, the worst possible outcome, the death of a teen. While many parents have done their utmost to provide an organized "safe" environment – with parent volunteers, controlled quantities of liquor, and on-site first aid – the fact remains that the risks at these all night "wet" or "damp" grad parties are far too high. Too often the fun turns to tragedy.

Having seen the fallout from these parties firsthand, Constable Ravi Gunasinghe of the Sidney, BC, RCMP states, "*Parents are justifying allowing minors to consume alcohol, some of these children being two years away from being able to legally purchase and consume alcohol. Hosts of these parties are also at risk of liability when allowing minors to consume alcohol on their property. So, aside from corrupting a minor, how many parents know just how much alcohol a given child can tolerate and how can a parent or other adult, determine when a child is no longer impaired or intoxicated? A person who drinks 12 ounces of alcohol throughout a ten-hour time frame at a party may not be intoxicated when they prepare to leave the event, but may still be impaired for several hours after. Potential consequences include verbal and physical violence, alcohol poisoning, introduction of other drugs, medical distress and impaired driving crashes"* – along with the possibility of liability and litigation issues for the adults involved.

The truth is *there is an alternative to risky parties* that not only reduces the risk and possible harms, but provides an exciting and memorable finalé that grads will not only want to attend, but will talk about for years to come. The solution is a safe, "dry" (non-alcoholic) After-Grad (AG) – an all-night, all-inclusive, controlled celebration where no one has to make a decision about using alcohol or drugs because it is taken completely out of the equation. Typically, an After-Grad follows the convocation ceremony and/or school-sponsored dinner/dance and can run anywhere from 9 pm through to 5 or 6 am – leaving no opportunity to join any other party that night.

This high energy and highly entertaining event can represent a new tradition that eliminates uncontrolled underage drinking, driving under the influence of drugs or alcohol, and other high risk behaviours. It shows students that they are cared about and valued, and it sends a clear message that a sober celebration is not only encouraged and supported but can represent the time of their life not the end of their lifetime!

The secret to making this After-Grad truly successful and unforgettable is:

- ✓ a group of dedicated and caring adults,
- ✓ a supportive school community, and
- ✓ an event 'blueprint' that really works – which you have in this book, born as a result of five successful years of fabulous AG events!

I was fortunate during my 20 plus year career as a professional conference and event planner to enjoy a great deal of flexibility which allowed me to spend much of my time at home with my children. And having nurtured and now watched my three children graduate, I have experienced firsthand the angst and joy that comes with parenting teens as they navigate those final high school years, learn to drive, and begin to take responsibility for their own decisions, including how to spend their time on Friday night! It made sense and was a great fit for my organizational talents to lend my time and event planning expertise to our local high school as it made the shift to an all-night, safe, dry grad event, which we came to call the After-Grad.

The year our first teen was in grade 11, our high school, Parkland Secondary in Sidney, BC, was ready for some real change. In early 2005, Vice Principal Steve Newlove was thinking about grade 12 graduation day and how each year, a growing number of students were leaving the organized school dinner/dance for less organized beach or field parties, events that included underage drinking. In June, after that year's grad celebration had ended, Steve and a small group of parents and upcoming graduates came together to talk about an all-night, safe, "dry" and secure grad event.

In September, the grad executive for the upcoming 2006 graduation class (our daughter's class) gave their endorsement for a dry safe event. Together with some supportive parents and grade 12 grad executive students, Steve made his sales pitch at the Grad Parent Orientation presentation that October. He had the students onside which meant they could help sell the idea to their own parents. The students wanted an alternative to the field or beach party – and to make memories, a "night to remember" not one they would forget. It couldn't be boring or dull, it had to be exciting, interactive, and had to keep them busy and awake all night, after an already long and emotionally charged day. Everyone – parents, students and teachers – wanted the grads to have the time of their lives, in a safe and secure environment, and not risk their lives doing it. There were other successful dry grad events in BC and in Canada to look to for ideas and guidelines, and there was time – nine months to pull it all together. Parkland Secondary was up for the challenge!

So, when Steve and a very supportive graduating student's parent – Sharon Woods – invited me to meet and talk over some ideas, I walked in with an open mind. I had my own graduating daughter who I wanted to keep safe that night, and I had the advantage of those many years of corporate conference planning and event organizing on my side.

We had the desire and enthusiasm, now we just had to figure out what they would do all night!

And with that, the "All-Night Parkland Safe After-Grad" was born, out of a desire to provide our students with an all-night event they would never forget, in a safe and secure environment they wouldn't want to leave.

Today, as we move into 2011 and our sixth year, our all-night event has become a tremendous success story. Boasting over 96% attendance in each year, the After-Grad has become part of the culture at Parkland Secondary, a real tradition and one that graduates are excited about in September and grateful for in June!

Parkland Secondary's AG event has inspired other high schools in British Columbia, and I have been corresponding with school representatives in other provinces to provide advice and planning suggestions. Parents have invited me to make presentations and to teach our 'system' for planning a successful event, and since I can't be at every school, it made sense to create a book and a website that could be. The book and its website are the most effective way for me to explain the process step-by-step, and provide parents, grads and teachers with all the checklists, schedules, forms and other tools. I believe, that by following the system, your school will be well on its way to hosting a fantastic After-Grad that will exceed everyone's expectations.

> *"Our school community greatly supports this parent-sponsored evening as it provides a safe and dry graduation activity. It is comforting to parents and school staff knowing our graduates are safe on their graduation evening."*
>
> — Bob Lee, principal, & Steve Newlove, vice principal, Parkland Secondary School

How to use this book

My intent in writing the book was to provide an easy-to-use and informative resource, as well as a support as you work on a project that may seem daunting at times. I hope that some of the ideas inspire you, and that the information will help you stay on track, while making it a manageable and enjoyable process, one that you can be proud to be a part of, and one that helps create a truly memorable event for your graduating class.

Each year, when we begin our After-Grad work in September, we look forward to having ten months in which to create a truly memorable event. Whether you have the luxury of time or have just picked this book up in March, I will take you through the process from beginning to end, providing you with a step-by-step approach. I use the same approach to every event, breaking down the project into small, very manageable chunks. This is especially important because if you are like me, you already have a job, a family, a life... and you are working on the After-Grad in your "spare" time.

This book does not make any promises or provide you with any guarantees that your event will be successful, that nothing will go awry, or that you won't encounter challenges along the way or during the event. What it does provide you with is a framework, a place to start, and a process to follow – one that works, and one that has brought us tremendous success for the past 5 years.

As most After-Grad events are designed and operated by a volunteer committee or

Dry Grad Society, this book has been designed using a committee approach, listing various tasks and duties assigned to sub-committees and coordinator positions. We've used the following icons to identify the recommended eight positions and sub-committees:

Chair	Communications & Publicity Co-ordinator	Finances Co-ordinator	Volunteer Committee	Transportation, Operations & Safety Committee	Decorating, Food & Beverage Committee	Entertainment, Games & Contests Committee	Fundraising & Prizes Committee

Within this book, each monthly section begins with a calendar filled with action items for that month, listed by committee or coordinator, along with a suggested weekly order for completing those items. You may, of course, complete the "action items" in any order you like, however, keep in mind that other committees or individuals may depend on your completing one task before they can move on to another on their own list, hence the calendar concept. Follow the book, or move along at your own pace, include some, all or none of the suggestions, but however you decide to make it happen, the monthly calendar will serve as a reminder of where you are in the process, and while your event may look very different than ours, many of the components and 'action items' will most certainly be on your list too.

Keep in mind that our event examples are based on a group size of 200; you will need to adjust if you have a smaller or larger graduating class or if your event includes multiple schools.

Along with the monthly action items, I have also included samples of the forms I use each year to help make the process easier. They are all available to download from the website – www.safegradevent.com

- ✓ You may decide to simply use them as a guide, and create your own forms, or
- ✓ download the Word and Excel versions and change the sample information to suit your unique event needs, or
- ✓ download the PDF version if you don't have Word or Excel.

✓ How about uploading the forms onto an online sharing site so that everyone has access to them and you can revise them as you move along? Some forms are used by more than one committee so sharing them can be a very useful tool, especially the calendar which can be updated and seen by everyone at all times.

We've learned a lot along the way, and are pleased to share it all with you. And, remember that while this graduation year will go by far too quickly, the memories of the After-Grad you are creating, really will last a lifetime. It's such a worthwhile and meaningful journey, and I wish you a truly successful and unforgettable event!

"Linda has established the 'after-grad template' for new parent organizers to go forward with. And not just for Parkland, but other high schools are learning from her talents and her experience."

— Heather McAughtrie, Catering and
Conference Manager, University of Victoria
Students' Society

Making it UNFORGETTABLE!

What makes an After-Grad unforgettable? Community support; a safe & secure environment; exciting, interactive and fun entertainment; fabulous food & beverages; and fantastic prizes. Add to that mix: a group of dedicated and supportive parents to organize and run the event, and you have the makings of a truly memorable After-Grad. And while no two events are ever exactly the same, there are certain components that are a "must" for an After-Grad to be truly unforgettable!

COMMUNITY SUPPORT

Whether it's the school administration, grads and their parents, or the community at large, you cannot go it alone. A safe, dry After-Grad is a daunting prospect for anyone who is trying to run their first event, and you need support. You must spread the "positive" message of the value and importance of the event, and what it means to everyone involved.

SAFETY & SECURITY

An After-Grad must take into consideration the well-being of everyone in attendance – systems and measures need to be established to ensure the best possible environment. Having both a Security and a Wellness Team as part of your event ensures the necessary level of safety, security and comfort.

It makes sense to partner with your local police department and/or fire department, a professional security firm, and medical personnel including doctors, nurses, first responders, and emergency medical support/paramedics. A professional security firm will have their own thoughts on how to handle the registration and security check, but be sure to also make your expectations known along with any unique concerns or considerations related to your guest group.

ENTERTAINMENT

For an After-Grad to be the one "party" that Grads *want* to attend, the entertainment has to be exciting, interactive, energetic, awesome, cool, amazing, fun, outrageous, memorable…. you get the idea – they must be "entertained"!

To ensure the highest level of enjoyment, we believe you need to include a range of activities and different kinds of entertainment. This generation of teens is used to a high level of interaction and instant gratification. A selection from the following list of activities will go a long way to keeping your grads and their guests "engaged" for the entire six or more hours:

- ✓ roaming and stationary "live" entertainment – magicians, jugglers, fortune tellers, tattoo artists, caricaturists, actors, dancers, street performers, stilt walkers
- ✓ performances – comedians, hypnotists, skits, cultural performances
- ✓ games – video games (*XBOX 360, Rock Band, DDR, Nintendo Wii*), arcade games (*Pac-Man*, pinball, simulators, sports games), air hockey, foosball, billiards, life-size board games (chess, checkers, *TWISTER*), casino games, bingo, darts)
- ✓ contests – limbo, hula hoop, relays
- ✓ music (a very important component) – dancing and dance contests, music videos, karaoke, live bands, open microphone, battle of the bands
- ✓ sports and inflatables – hockey, swimming, tennis, volleyball, soccer, Sumo wrestling, climbing walls, bungee run, obstacle courses, gladiator games, jousting, bouncy castles (you read that right)

- ✓ photographs and videos – videographers, photographers, photo booths, digital photo loops, full length movies, television shows
- ✓ souvenir T-shirts are the number one After-Grad souvenir. Every grad receives a plain white T-shirt, a coloured fabric/permanent marker and they spend hours writing and signing shirts as a permanent memory of their grad year and great night.

FOOD & BEVERAGE

Teens eat a lot! My teens eat even more! An After-Grad has to keep grads well fed and well hydrated. This keeps headaches and fatigue at bay and helps the group stay energized – it's a long night. It has to be easy and convenient to grab a bite or they will avoid the buffets. So make it easy for them by serving foods that appeal to teens, are healthy with an emphasis on fresh fruit, vegetables and proteins, and less dessert or sugary items. Choose food items that are small, easy-to-snack-on finger foods, that don't require cutlery, and can be eaten quickly. Offer foods that they can walk around with, eat while they are in a line-up and that aren't too messy. Include lots of bottled water, in lots of places, to keep them hydrated without a lot of added sugar. Offer a limited selection of fruit juices, soft drinks and coffee, only in the early hours, and definitely disallow energy drinks.

Why no energy drinks? The Canadian Medical Association Journal raised alarm in July 2010 that 'energy drinks' are potentially addictive and contain very high levels of caffeine, and may be crossing the line into the 'drug' category.

PRIZES

Prizes are a huge draw for an After-Grad. Each year, we have given away thousands of dollars in prizes and tuitions/bursaries – gathered through fundraising efforts, a raffle and local business support. Each and every attending grad has received a prize along with chances to win an additional 10 to 25 larger, more expensive items including the latest electronics and computers, and tuitions/bursaries for post secondary education. We even gave away a car in our first year (an older car, refurbished free of charge) and many schools give vehicles away as their grand prize.

EVENT FLOW

One of the best ways to keep everyone present and engaged is to "build up" the excitement throughout the night. We have done that by making most of our entertainment available from the event start, then introducing "live" performances such as bands and hypnotists in the wee hours (a typically "flat" time for the event), and finishing up with the Prize Draw, where you must be in attendance to win.

> *"To this day I remember every detail of the After-Grad because alcohol was not a part of it."*
>
> — Rhys, graduate

BUILDING THE EXCITEMENT

ere's a description of a theoretical After-Grad that you can use to "paint a picture" of what's possible if your parents, school administrators and grads have no experience with a safe, dry, unforgettable event.

YOU ARE INVITED TO…

An Unforgettable After-Grad

As you leave your graduation dinner/dance with your fellow graduates and guests, a parent volunteer checks your name off the attendance list and hands you a coloured wristband – allowing entry to an unforgettable all-night fabulous experience. You make your way to the awaiting double-decker bus. Onboard, finding a selection of coloured bandanas, beachcomber hats, sunglasses and flashing rings, you pick out something that goes with your outfit, and sit back and relax, while your tour guide takes you on a little journey to your 'island paradise' where the party is waiting!

Everything is black outside – it's 10.30 pm after all. As you listen to the tour guide announce all of the great things there are to do tonight, in the distance you can just make out the edge of a huge flashing 'Welcome to Paradise' sign, and then more lights, hundreds of lights, the building is aglow. Arriving in style, walk the red carpet walkway, under a lighted archway of flowers, over the bridge and through the doors, all while the tropical music is blasting through the air. A mermaid hands you a lei, and a pirate – parrot and all – hands you some gold doubloons from his latest ship raid.

Toting your change of clothes, you make your way through the main entrance doors, pass through the security check, where you are met by more pirates (friendly ones, thankfully) and two local police officers who pat down everyone and may use a breathalyser (don't want any alcohol or drugs spoiling this once-in-a-lifetime party!). Next, three merry buccaneers serve everyone a 'welcome mocktail' along with a canapé or two. Leaving your personal belongings at the coat check, you head to the commemorative T-shirt table and the signing begins – it's a sight to see, hundreds of grads, all signing their fellow classmates' shirts, with thoughts and expressions about graduation, friendship and future wishes, creating a souvenir to last a lifetime. Donning your T-shirt, beachcomber hat and lei, you are 'in theme' and ready to try out one of the over 23 activities available tonight.

A walk through the tropical lounge and it's the karaoke you hit first (who says you don't sound like Celine Dion?). Behind the karaoke, there is a continuous loop of After-Grad digital images showing… oh and look, now there's one of Celine. Get inside the photobooth and take a picture strip of you and your friends, play a little pinball or Pac Man, take a stab at foosball or air hockey, and then a little competition among friends playing the XBOX or Wii. Among the palm trees, fishing nets and sea shells, the buffet table is loaded, so grab a little something on your way out, maybe a mini-wrap, some veggies and a bottle of water, and then it's off to see what else the evening has in store. Just before you head out, game to try the limbo or hula hoop contest, anyone?

Moving along the hallway, you find a hot dog vendor and fresh hot popcorn – hmmm, maybe later, more to do first. The magician is doing some unbelievable sleight-of-hand tricks or how about a caricature of you and your best friend, one that will last forever? You can leave the finished masterpiece at the coat check, and then move on to the temporary tattoo stand where you can have your arm airbrushed with a beautiful tropical flower. A little further down the hall, join in the beach relay contest, and then head straight into the casino.

This noisy place is filled with the sounds of tropically-clad dealers and lots of hopeful players, looking for Lady Luck. Huge tropical palm trees, grass-skirted tables, and all kinds of casino games await, so why not try your hand at blackjack, the wheel, poker, or maybe a little bingo or a game of billiards, all with faux money and real fun. Another buffet means more snacks, a bottle of juice, and now it's time for a little dancing in the nightclub.

The nightclub is bouncing with lots of flashing lights, videos playing on floating screens, and glow sticks for everyone. Dancers are joining in the contests and requesting their favourite dance tunes. It won't be long now until the live band takes over and after that you won't want to miss the hypnotist's performance.

You are back in the main hallway, fresh hot pizza is being made to order, and friends are playing Rock Band. It's been hours since you first arrived, so how about a little break – you can freshen up with the washroom amenities that have been provided, drop into the wellness room if you need to rest, or head down to the buffet for a hot cup of coffee and a little dessert. This has been an amazing night, and it's not over yet.

The hypnotist is ready to take the stage, so back to the nightclub to enjoy his performance and to watch your grad class make fools of themselves, or chickens, or rock stars! And just when you think it doesn't get better than this, the chicken-fool-rock-star performance is over, and you are waiting for the grand finale, the prize draw worth thousands, and hopefully a nice little souvenir to take home – new laptop anyone?

Still in the nightclub, this becomes the final stop on this amazing After-Grad journey. Everyone, and I mean everyone, is gathered together, for the big prize draw. There are hundreds of prizes, and every grad in attendance will go home tonight with at least one prize – maybe a local restaurant or gas gift card. And then, everyone's name is thrown back in the raffle drum for the really big draw – for the latest electronics or a shopping spree, and maybe even a college tuition prize. It's been a winning night for everyone, and now it's time to gather up your prizes, grab a granola bar and juice to go, and make your way to the buses, for the early morning ride home. It's 5 am and you have just had the night of your life – along with your entire grad class, the friends you will never forget, and all in a safe, secure, energized, and fun-filled environment – unforgettable!

SEPTEMBER

September marks the beginning of the school year, an exciting and busy time. As a parent, my first week is usually filled with signing forms, paying fees, adjusting to class schedules and developing new "waking teens" strategies, leaving little time or inclination to think about graduation!

If your school already has an established AG committee or Dry Grad Society, it may take a few weeks to get it started. If your school's parent group has never offered a dry, safe After-Grad, then it's time to take the first step in establishing a new tradition by presenting the idea to the school administration, parents and grad students, and getting them to embrace the idea and "buy" in. One of the challenges of selling the "dry" idea to resistant grads and oftentimes parents, is a society view where some parents and graduates believe that it is a "rite of passage" to include alcohol on graduation night and where fun equates to liquor. And while there may be some resistance at your school, most parents will want to be a part of an event that keeps their children safe, and their own sleep intact. You may not have any elected committee positions as of yet, so you may have to be the voice, and assume the responsibilities of the chair, while waiting for the formal creation of an AG committee.

SEPTEMBER – ACTION ITEMS

Week	Chair	Communications & Publicity Co-ordinator	Finances Co-ordinator	Volunteer Committee	Transportation, Operations & Safety Committee	Decorating, Food & Beverage Committee	Entertainment, Games & Contests Committee	Fundraising & Prizes Committee
Week 1	Meet with School Administration & Confirm Dates							
	Meet Last Year's AG Committee							
Week 2								
Week 3	Attend Parent Advisory Group/ Council (PAC) Meeting							
Week 4	Create Initial Parent Contact List							

Sample "Action Items – September" is available as a PDF document or an Excel document at www.safegradevent.com/tools/forms/actionitemsseptember

 CHAIR

Meet with School Administration & Confirm Dates – week one

A great place to begin your "dry grad" conversation is the principal's office (this time you *want* to be there!). If the option of a dry, safe After-Grad is a new concept for the school, then this is a great time to determine the level of support you can anticipate and to discuss moving forward.

If the date of the graduation ceremony and/or dinner/dance has already been set, then this may become your event date, if you want to have the After-Grad take place on the same night. Even if the After-Grad takes place on another date, it's important to know the actual graduation date as it may impact your planning.

Meet Last Year's AG Committee – week one

If your school had an After-Grad last year, now is the time to meet last year's chair and to discuss moving forward with this year's event and striking a new committee. Be sure to review the committee notes from the previous event as these will help create an even more successful event this time around. If that committee is having a September debrief meeting, ask to attend, so you can hear about the event first-hand.

Attend Parent Advisory Group/Council (PAC) Meeting – week three

Attend the first parent group/council meeting of the year, and ask for a spot on the agenda to be devoted to a discussion about After-Grad. Opening a conversation with this group will hopefully garner their support as they are a group of already dedicated parents who are giving time and energy to the well-being of the students and their school community and who will likely support a healthy and safe event for graduates. The council can be your greatest support as well as a source of funding – use this meeting to inquire about their requirements for funding requests. We have been generously supported each year by our PAC and have received monies for both the event and bursaries.

The first council meeting may be advertised through the school website or newsletter, so this is also a good opportunity to request parents to attend the meeting and to mention that the After-Grad will be on the agenda. It may also be worthwhile to include school administrators at this first meeting, to show their support and to include them in some meaningful discussion with parents who will be invited to share ideas and concerns. Ask your school-police liaison or other local police representative to come to the meeting, to speak to the statistics on drinking and driving, along with the legalities and liabilities associated with the alternative of planning/participating in a "wet grad".

Talk about the *advantages* of a Dry Grad – it's an all-inclusive, all-night, amazing party that creates lasting, lifelong memories – the entire grad class is welcome, and they won't forget this night – in fact they will still be talking about it at the 10-year reunion. Be prepared to share any information you have available that will help parents understand why this event is so important, and how they too can successfully operate a dry, safe After-Grad. If other schools in your area have held successful dry grad events, ask them to share those successes. Those committees are a valuable resource. When we started working on our first event in late 2005, another local school (Claremont Secondary) shared a great deal of their information, including their challenges and suggestions for change, which saved us time and allowed us to avoid similar pitfalls in our first event. We have since gone on to share our successes and recommendations with other schools, ensuring that the message continues to be spread.

And, if people still want more proof, offer up some of the testimonials in the book – quotes from real grads who attended our all-night event, many of them who would have been at a booze-included "wet grad" if that had been their only alternative.

Use this council meeting as an opportunity to secure parent email addresses that can be used to build a comprehensive data base, which will enable you to continue to connect with parents and provide information throughout the year. Student emails can be gathered by the grad class executive once their student grad committee is up and running. You can also use this time to solicit parents' help for possible inclusion in an AG committee, and to distribute Volunteer Forms to interested parents.

Once you have an AG committee, you will be able to hold monthly meetings, while staying in touch with the parent council and reporting to them each month on your progress, as well as requesting any assistance you may require.

Note: If your school/PAC wants your Dry Grad Committee to exist and operate completely separate of the school, you may need to create a non-profit society – see the Resource Section at the website for more information.

A sample "Volunteer Form" is available in Appendix – Forms, and as a PDF document or a Word document at www.safegradevent.com/tools/forms/volunteer

Create Initial Parent Contact List – week four

Use any Volunteer Forms you may have collected to create a contact list or database that can be used for your email distribution and that will later form the basis for a volunteer data base for the volunteer sub-committee.

> *"The After-Grad was an amazing time for all of us grads to get together, while being safe. A lot of memories were remembered that night while looking back on our 13 years together."*
>
> — Jesse, graduate

OCTOBER

Although it may seem as though year end and the event are light years away, time is going to pass quickly. There are a number of items you can take care of during these first few months, so use this time to strike your committees, determine roles, and to determine the kind of event your graduates want.

OCTOBER – ACTION ITEMS

Week	Chair	Communications & Publicity Co-ordinator	Finances Co-ordinator	Volunteer Committee	Transportation, Operations & Safety Committee	Decorating, Food & Beverage Committee	Entertainment, Games & Contests Committee	Fundraising & Prizes Committee
Week 1	Participate in School Grad Meeting							
Week 2	Research & Select Venue	Create AG Website or School Website AG Page						
	Develop AG Committee or Establish a Dry Grad Society							
Week 3	Prepare AG article	Update Parent Contact List						
Week 4	AG Committee Meeting	AG Committee Meeting	AG Committee Meeting	AG Committee Meeting	AG Committee Meeting	AG Committee Meeting	AG Committee Meeting	AG Committee Meeting

Sample "Action Items – October" is available as a PDF document or an Excel document at www.safegradevent.com/tools/forms/actionitemsoctober

 CHAIR

Participate in School Grad Meeting – week one

In early October, our school administration often hosts a meeting or presentation for the grade 12/ grad parents. Attending, and even better, joining in this meeting is a great way to introduce the After-Grad concept and to invite parents to volunteer to participate in an AG committee and/or the event. We have been fortunate each year to be invited to speak at the presentation, which has gone a long way to providing credibility for the event as well as showing the full support of the administration. And, what better chance than this to speak to an almost entire grad parent group.

Have your Volunteer Forms available once again (never miss an opportunity to solicit volunteers or support), and mention that you need the email addresses to keep the communication flowing for the next nine months. This is an important task to complete while you have so many available parents as the school may not be permitted to provide parent contact information/email addresses due to the *Freedom of Information and Protection of Privacy Act* or similar legislation.

The sample "Volunteer Form" is available in Appendix – Forms, and as a PDF document or a Word document at www.safegradevent.com/tools/forms/volunteer

Research & Select Venue – week two

While you have not yet established an AG Committee, it's important that a venue be researched and selected now if at all possible. June is such a busy month for all graduating classes and you may be competing with other schools for venue space, dates and times. Even booking a venue on a tentative basis is worthwhile, while you wait to confirm your final committee members. And, if your school knows the graduation ceremony dates for several forthcoming years, consider booking the After-Grad venue for a few years in a row, even tentatively. It will be a great help to future committees.

Often the After-Grad will take place on the same date as another school-sponsored graduation event (ceremony, dinner/dance, etc.). Keep this in mind as you select a venue as the proximity of the two locations is an important consideration for timing and transportation.

There are a limited number of venues that work well for this type of event, and not all venues have enough space or facilities to accommodate the various components that are integral to an After-Grad. Most commonly used venues include: a recreation or leisure centre, a school or college/university student facility, an amusement or theme park, a cruise boat, a sports arena, or a convention centre. Smaller groups may be able to have an After-Grad at the school, using several spaces within the building.

To assist you in making your venue selection, I have included a series of questions you may want to ask in a venue meeting or phone call. If you have time and access to the venue, it is worthwhile to do a "walk through." You can then describe the venue to the other committee members in the AG committee meeting later this month and you will have the information you need in order to make your final decision. You may need to sign a contract early on and provide a deposit, so you want to be sure you have selected the right venue for your event. Some venues may provide a discount once they know this is a not-for-profit event and most will confirm a price that they are willing to hold for the following year, so be sure to ask.

It is helpful to have the following information available to the venue so that they can provide an accurate quote:

- ✓ Your group size. The school administrator can provide you with the number of grads in this year's class. If you are permitting guests, allow an additional 10 to 20% extra which you will need to add to the number to the grad class. Some After-Grads permit only the graduating class to attend; others include guests if they are

attending the same school (i.e., "dates" or "friends" from a lower grade); and still others allow guests from other schools if they are within the same community.
- ✓ The number of volunteers and suppliers you anticipate having onsite during the event (allow 25 to 30 for a group of 200, or 15% of the total guest number).

The sample "Venue Questions" are available in Appendix – Forms, and as a PDF document or a Word document at www.safegradevent.com/tools/forms/venuequestions

Develop AG Committee or Establish a Dry Grad Society – week two

Using your email addresses, set up a meeting date for interested parents, so that you can begin to form an AG committee. At this early date, you may not have someone who has stepped up to chair an AG committee – it may be a PAC or parent council member that starts this process.

Sometimes it takes a few weeks for the students in the graduating class to create an executive group and they typically set a number of things in motion including the theme selection, so be patient and work on those items that you can while waiting for the graduates to get started with their own committees.

While your AG committee can include as many sub-committees as you like, one proven route is to have five sub-committees along with three key positions (the chair, plus finance and communications coordinators) who assist with the organization and running of the overall committee. Within that group of five sub-committees you will involve lots of parent volunteers to get the various jobs done. When the executive meets, you (as chair) need only consider the schedules of 8 individuals – you, the two other key positions and the heads of the five sub-committees. You can later divide the budget in a similar way.

Although some schools group and divide up the responsibilities in slightly different ways, the following list of positions and sub-committees represents an efficient way to organize the responsibilities/duties:

Chair (position)

- ✓ Establish meeting timeline, set agendas, chair meetings
- ✓ Report to PAC, school administration
- ✓ Maintenance of overall budget
- ✓ Liaise with school administration, parents, grad class
- ✓ Venue research selection
- ✓ Research and purchase of Event/Liability Insurance

Communications & Publicity Coordinator (position)

- ✓ Record and distribute AG meeting minutes
- ✓ Distribute AG updates to PAC, school and grad parents
- ✓ Create and/or distribute AG Survey, Attendance Lists, Agreements, Event Binder, Bus Script
- ✓ Publicity plan and media coverage
- ✓ Thank-yous and gifts
- ✓ Website creation/maintenance
- ✓ Printing and signage

Finance Coordinator (position)

- ✓ [If you are organizing as a non-profit society] Set up of society; file society annual report
- ✓ Preparation of event budget and budget analysis
- ✓ Accounts receivable – deposits, cheques, reporting, statement preparation, grant/aid applications
- ✓ Accounts payable – suppliers, rental companies, entertainers
- ✓ Prize draw – cash prizes, bursaries, tuitions
- ✓ Raffle and fundraising reconciliation and reporting

Volunteer Sub-committee

- ✓ Volunteer recruitment and ongoing communications (40 to 50 volunteers for a group of 200 to 250 grads, and 300 for a group of 850 to 900)
- ✓ Coordination and assignment of volunteer event positions and Volunteer grid
- ✓ Volunteer meeting and training sessions including casino, etc.
- ✓ Liaise with local police force, medical/wellness team
- ✓ Coat check, bag check, change of clothes check/distribution
- ✓ Entrance identification and distribution of ID wristbands
- ✓ Volunteer security, escorts

 ### Transportation, Operations & Safety Sub-committee

- ✓ Delivery/pickup of event components
- ✓ Organization of transportation for grads/guests to/from event
- ✓ Bus escorts, novelty placement, themed commentary
- ✓ Event cleanup, recycling, litter/garbage pickup
- ✓ Coordination of Wellness and Security Team
- ✓ Liaise with suppliers

 ### Decorating, Food & Beverage Sub-committee

- ✓ Research and select a Food & Beverage Provider (chair may assist with this)
- ✓ Secure rentals for decor items
- ✓ Setup/teardown of all decoration/food & beverage items at the event
- ✓ Menu selection and floorplan creation
- ✓ Coordination of incoming F&B items, such as specialty items, vending machines, bottled water, hot dog, cotton candy, popcorn machines, etc.

Entertainment, Games & Contests Sub-committee

- ✓ Research and secure entertainers/performers
- ✓ Research and secure entertainment, games, contests
- ✓ Negotiate entertainer/performer contracts, deposits, tech needs
- ✓ Setup/teardown of electronic, technical and AV equipment
- ✓ Purchase T-shirts, novelites and contest props
- ✓ Onsite handling of entertainment and performers

 ### Fundraising & Prizes Sub-committee

- ✓ Gaming licenses, raffle/prize draw, event ticket printing
- ✓ Research opportunities and develop fundraising campaign
- ✓ Collection, purchase, organization of prizes, distribution at the event

Getting together on a monthly basis is important – a committee meeting later in each month gives you an opportunity to complete a fair amount of work, and then prepare for the next month's action items list. While you may have a large number of parents involved in committees and providing help in many ways, I recommend that you include only the key positions and sub-committee leaders at the monthly meetings. This will mean a much faster meeting and decisions will be made more easily. The larger the group, the more opportunity to get bogged down. (This advice comes from years of committee work.) Establish a monthly meeting time and location that works for all and get started!

Prepare AG Article – week three

In order to garner additional support from the school and larger community, it may be worthwhile to write to the local newspaper and/or community organizations about the importance of supporting the After-Grad. Starting to spread the word helps establish or reinforce a tradition in the community for this event, and may open the door for fundraising and solicitation to local business later on in the process. If there is a communications person in place, this task can be assigned to him/her, and/or shared with the chair.

COMMUNICATIONS & PUBLICITY

Create AG Website or School Website AG Page – week two

Many Dry Grad societies or committees have developed their own websites, while other groups take over a page or an area within their school's website. This is such a valuable communication avenue so, if at all possible, try to enlist a technically-able and interested individual within the grad parent group who can develop and maintain this site.

Have a look at other committees' websites to get an idea of the kinds of information they include and remember to keep the site current, and post your monthly meeting minutes here for everyone to read.

Some grad classes have a Facebook page and you may want to have access so you can see what grads are saying about a safe, dry, After-Grad and so you can include updates and information about the event – it may help to promote the concept here as this is where many grads 'meet'.

Update Parent Contact List – week three

Following any grad parent presentations this month, you may have gathered some new volunteer forms or email addresses to update your contact list. This is the list that will become so important when it's time to start putting together a Volunteer Grid for the event.

AG Committee Meeting – week four

Remember to record minutes of these meetings (this is the job of the communications person), as these will provide a guide for the current sub-committees. The minutes will also form the basis of an important file that can be used from year to year for future committees. Once your society/parent group has operated a successful and memorable AG event, there is no going back, so next year's parent group will want to benefit from your expertise!

Use this first meeting to:

✓ determine areas of interest elect or appoint positions including the chair, finance and communications, and to build the sub-committees.

✓ review next month's calendar of action items

✓ report on action items that have been worked on already, including the parent/grad meeting/presentation and any other meetings with school administrators

✓ report on the venue selection process and any decision/selection made.

"Finally there is help for those parent committees struggling with the organizing of their school's dry grad. I have worked with hundreds of grads over the past 25 years and seen the success and importance of celebrating the once-in-a-lifetime graduation in a safe and organized environment. Linda Hunter's book is what every grad committee needs – easy to use and comprehensive. Get it, you'll use it and you'll be glad you did!"

— Robert Mesmer, America's Grad Hypnotist
direct from Princess Cruise Lines

NOVEMBER

November may be the start of cooler weather, but it's also when event preparation starts to heat up. Having established your sub-committees, you can get down to surveying the grads, determining a theme, and developing a working budget. This month is about research, sourcing suppliers and building the actual event. I try to accomplish a lot in November, because December includes school vacation and a busy holiday season. If you find yourself getting behind by the end of November, you can always use a few days in December to catch up so you are ready to move forward again in January.

NOVEMBER – ACTION ITEMS

Week	Chair	Communications & Publicity Co-ordinator	Finances Co-ordinator	Volunteer Committee	Transportation, Operations & Safety Committee	Decorating, Food & Beverage Committee	Entertainment, Games & Contests Committee	Fundraising & Prizes Committee
Week 1		Create & Distribute AG Surveys			Venue Walk Through			
Week 2	Secure Event/Liability Insurance	Remind Grads of Survey Due Date	Create AG Account/Books			Research & Select F&B Provider		
Week 3		Collect AG Surveys		Create Volunteer Data Base				Research Fundraising Opportunities & Develop Initial Plan
		Tabulate Survey Results & Prepare Survey Report						
		Distribute Survey Report to AG Committee & Grad Exec						Create an F&P Contact List
Week 4	Develop a Theme Concept & Event Flow	Develop Publicity & Print Plan	Develop a Working Budget		Source & Secure Suppliers	Source & Secure Suppliers	Source & Secure Suppliers	Source & Secure Suppliers
		Create Supplier Contact List			Secure Wellness & Security Team	Develop Quote Sheet	Develop Quote Sheet	Develop Quote Sheet
					Develop Quote Sheet			
	AG Committee Meeting	AG Committee Meeting	AG Committee Meeting	AG Committee Meeting	AG Committee Meeting	AG Committee Meeting	AG Committee Meeting	AG Committee Meeting

Sample "Action Items – November" is available as a PDF document or an Excel document at www.safegradevent.com/tools/forms/actionitemsnovember

# CHAIR

Secure Event/Liability Insurance – week two

As the various sub-committees are now sourcing their suppliers, this is good time to source an insurance provider for the event. The sub-committees will need to provide you with a list of the types of security and safety measures being put in place as well as the types of entertainment and performances being researched, so the insurer has a good idea of what your event includes.

Purchasing event liability insurance is a "must do" for the event. While you put the measures and systems in place so that all goes well, anything can happen, from an entertainer slipping on a spilled drink in the hallway, to a more serious grad incident resulting from a medical condition, so be sure to source and purchase the insurance you need to suit your particular event's requirements. Ask your insurer questions, and know your coverage details. And be sure that your suppliers all carry insurance as well.

A policy may be purchased by a Dry Grad Society, a school Parent Council or a Parent Grad Committee – in other words the entity that is responsible for the event. And by doing this in November, you will know the cost of the insurance as this is a hard cost that must be included in the budget. If you have not yet established a Society or Parent Group, ask the insurer for your options while you still have time to take the necessary steps to put the optimal insurance in place.

Check your local insurance companies to find one that offers this type of insurance and you can source on the web as well. We were able to secure economical insurance for our BC event from a company headquartered in Alberta.

Develop a Theme Concept & Event Flow – week four

With the returned surveys (see Communications & Publicity, week one, page 40), hopefully a theme has emerged. Creating a theme concept is like painting a "picture" of the event's overall look and feel. We have always tried to incorporate the theme throughout the entire event, from start to finish and have it show up in as many places as possible. We look for ways to incorporate the theme in each venue space, with the live performers and even the volunteers (they can dress the part), in the movie we show and the arcade games we select. It's important to develop the theme concept or at least some theme ideas so that the sub-committees who are researching suppliers know the theme they are working with – especially the decorating team.

It may be more efficient to develop a theme concept and event flow as a group, so consider having your AG meeting prior to sub-committees sourcing and securing suppliers.

One of easiest ways to build your theme concept is to brainstorm every idea or thought that comes to mind for a particular theme, and capture them all. Once you have them recorded, divide up the ideas into the various event categories and/or the rooms/spaces you will be using. The examples below illustrate two of our previous themes – New York City in 2008, and Tropical Paradise in 2010. We listed all of the ways that we could envision using the theme. It's a great list, and we didn't end up using every idea shown but it did give us a great starting place from which we could pick and choose what we thought might have the greatest impact, and that we could afford. We organized the list by sub-committee or event category, to ensure that every aspect of the event was in some way reflecting the theme, and then those ideas went to the applicable sub-committee for further budget research and quotes.

Theme Concept – "NEW YORK CITY"

- ✓ Tour guides on buses – describing the areas of New York they will see tonight – Broadway Avenue, Central Parkland, Studio 54, and New York's hottest Casino
- ✓ Volunteer casino dealers dressed like roaring 1920s "gangsters" with fedoras, etc.
- ✓ Volunteer parents in flapper outfits serving food trays in the casino
- ✓ Sandwich sign walker, Broadway playbills (what's going on tonight)

Transportation, Operations, Safety

- ✓ Set up the buses as New York City tour buses

 ### Decorating, Food & Beverage

- ✓ Novelties on the buses; feather boas, diamond rings, sunglasses for the girls, gangster hats, fedoras and black shades for the guys
- ✓ Flashing & twinkle lights, searchlight, red carpet, a skyline
- ✓ New York marquee sign to read, "And now playing, Parkland's 2008 After-Grad"
- ✓ A centre fountain or bird bath, old fashioned lamp standards, park benches, trees, outdoor garbage cans – in Central Parkland
- ✓ *Studio 54* sign outside the nightclub, disco ball, glow sticks and table toys
- ✓ Main Concourse set up to look like a New York Street – street signs, a flashing stop light, manhole covers, sign to the subway, a phone booth, Brooklyn Bridge or New York skyline in the background

 ### Entertainment, Games & Contests

- ✓ Corner karaoke stage, maybe a sign "Music/Concert in the Park"
- ✓ Mix the arcade/video games in amongst the trees
- ✓ Possibly a picture loop – the grad photos mixed in with famous New York images
- ✓ Roaring 1920s casino, with retro New York posters, gangster dealers
- ✓ Jazz music in the background – upbeat cool jazz, reflecting 1920s jazz era
- ✓ A screen running silent films – Charlie Chaplin was big in the 1920s
- ✓ DJ with smoke machine, light show, large screen running videos
- ✓ Street vendors and performers, like the T-shirt table, the pizza place, the popcorn machine, a hot dog vendor, T-shirt sales table, magician, artists, tattoo artists, mime, etc.

Theme Concept – "TROPICAL PARADISE"

- ✓ Bus escorts dressed in "tropical" outfits
- ✓ Bus escorts acting as tour guides – describing the areas of Paradise they will see tonight – the boardwalk, poolside, the nightclub, the casino
- ✓ A mermaid handing out leis upon arrival
- ✓ Volunteer pirates handing out coins, telling jokes, calling the bingo game
- ✓ Servers in tropical sundresses, grass skirts, sunglasses and flip flops
- ✓ Casino dealers in loud flowered shirts, shades and straw beach hats

Transportation, Operations, Safety

- ✓ Set the buses up as shuttles similar to those you take on vacation to your hotel

Decorating, Food & Beverage

- ✓ Novelty items on the buses, bandanas, straw hats, sunglasses, shell bracelets
- ✓ Outside: palm trees, loungers, beach balls, bridge/dock, lights, blue carpet
- ✓ Outdoor marquee sign: "Parkland 2010 – Welcome to Paradise!"
- ✓ Sand coloured table linens, pink flamingo centrepieces, tea lights, scattered sea shells and coloured stones, grass skirting on the buffet tables
- ✓ All entertainers in tropical dress
- ✓ Tropical mocktails with umbrellas, upon arrival, fresh fruit trays on the buffets
- ✓ Ice cream/snow cone machine, popcorn machine on the boardwalk

Entertainment, Games & Contests

- ✓ Tropical themed tattoos, caricatures done with a tropical background
- ✓ Tropical contests including beach relay, hula hoop, limbo

✓ Beach music in the nightclub, beach balls and coloured glow sticks
✓ A "beach/tropical" movie playing in the games room/lounge

Event Flow

Give some thought to the flow/ timing of your event, as I believe it can greatly impact the success of your After-Grad. Each year, we consider how best to keep the momentum going and how to continue to build the excitement throughout the entire night. If your event, like ours, runs through the night into the early morning, you will want to offer up your best live performances or "special events" during the morning hours of 2 and 4 am. This is typically a "flat time" when guests are tired, have already participated in a number of activities, and want something new to do or see to keep them going. This will have already been a long and emotional day, and many guests will have been awake since the early hours. If there is a moment when guests think about an early departure from the After-Grad, this is it – the wee hours of the morning. So we increase the excitement during that time, offering a 90-minute hypnotist/comedian performance and a live band if the grads have requested one, followed by our last activity, an amazing prize draw where guests must be in attendance in order to win, and where there's a prize for every grad – so no one leaves!

We generally offer our full program (with the exception of our live performances) from the very beginning of the event so that the event is in full swing when the guests arrive. This provides a huge selection of activities and keeps the energy high as the event moves through the first few hours. Some schools choose to stagger their program schedule, offering new entertainment every hour or so, however this can lead to long line-ups for those who are onsite at the beginning, and then longer line-ups later on, as new performers appear at the event and everyone wants a tattoo or caricature, for example.

Keep in mind also that many roaming entertainers/performers may have a minimum "call time" – the minimum performance time for which they charge. Many like to work a minimum of 4 hours, so we schedule our magician, tattoo artists, jugglers and caricaturists from the start at 11 pm through to 3 am. This gives everyone an opportunity to enjoy what these performers have to offer, and by the time they are winding down, our "live" performances are gearing up and grads are ready to recharge their battery, and take in something different.

We schedule live bands before our main feature entertainer (who for us and many other schools is a hypnotist or comedian). Once that performance is over, there is little time left in the event, so we move to our amazing prize draw, and an hour later, everyone is on buses, heading home. This schedule has proved so successful for us each year, that we have stayed with and recommended it to other schools.

The bonus is that while the live performances are taking place, our volunteer team gets busy and closes down areas that won't be used again, clears buffets, and moves food to the one remaining buffet in the performance area and prepares for the bus transfer.

Once created, you can present an "Event Flow" to grad parents and volunteers to help them envision what the event will look like hour by hour.

A sample "Event Flow" is available in Appendix – Forms and as a PDF document or as a Word document at www.safegradevent.com/tools/forms/eventflow

COMMUNICATIONS & PUBLICITY

Create & Distribute After-Grad Surveys – week one

One of the easiest and best ways to make it truly a "grad" event, is to have the grads plan the experience, by providing suggestions for a theme along with what they would like to see included. That's exactly what we did at Parkland in 2005 when we designed our first ever "After-Grad Survey." We put it to the students: "What would it take to make you want to attend an all-night, safe, dry, After-Grad party?" Although surveys traditionally don't have a big return rate, once you explain to grads that the way to truly own their event is to design it themselves – they tell you what they want, they complete the surveys. We would not begin the process each year without our survey; this event has to be about them

– the grads. And, when it comes to selling tickets to the event nine months from now, you will be able to honestly say that the grads created <u>their own event</u>!

Each year, we design our survey to include the most successful components from the previous year and we ask the grads what they want to include in "their" party. Theme suggestions and event components that prove popular from year to year are carried over and we include space for new suggestions for the current year.

Each year, more and more surveys are returned, and for the most part we are able to provide the majority of requested items. Most years, the grads want similar activities, but we do try to add a few surprises each year. In 2009 we added a photo booth which was so popular (900 images in 4 hours!) that we included it in our 2010 survey and it received enough votes to bring it back for our event. Before sending out the survey, check for any venue restrictions, since you don't want to make any promises you can't keep.

The survey template provided is just one example; you will need to customize it to your school and your grad class. If your venue is a sports & recreation centre, you may want to add sports activities and games along with inflatables (sumo wrestling, bungee run) to your survey.

In terms of an event theme, although it adds a whole other dimension to the event, and can make it much more exciting and visually appealing, it is not necessary to have one in order to produce a memorable and successful event – it's much more important to provide *entertainment*. For groups that select a recreation/leisure centre as their venue, a theme is often not even necessary – there is the built-in theme of "fun" and no additional theme concept is needed.

If your grads are interested in theming the event, I recommend that you help the grads out by suggesting theme choices (a good rule of thumb is to provide 4–6 choices from which to vote on). Each year, we provide a list of suggested themes and sometimes they come up with something completely different to add to the list, but either way, it's much easier to focus when you have a shorter list to review.

Some schools may choose to carry a theme throughout the entire graduating year and automatically attach it to the various events and activities associated with After-Grad; however a themed After-Grad can also stand alone as a single event. If the theme is carried throughout the year, it's important to determine what else is going on as there may be opportunities to cost share with suppliers, and you also want to ensure that there is no overlap between events.

Allow about 2 weeks for grads to return their completed surveys. Any longer, and they forget about them, leave them in their lockers or under their beds. An efficient route of return is to ask the school for a "drop off" location at the front office, or ask to share the Parent Council mailbox. This makes it convenient for grads, and you have a better chance of seeing some returned surveys. Alternatively, you can distribute the survey by email – you will need a list of grad email addresses, and permission from each grad to use that address. Grads can fill in the blanks and email the survey back to an After-Grad email address, set up by the chair or communications coordinator.

A sample "After-Grad Survey" is available in Appendix – Forms and as a PDF document or as a Word document at www.safegradevent.com/tools/forms/survey

Remind Grads of Survey Due Date – week two

Email a reminder to all grads for whom you have an email address. As well, many schools will often have an announcement monitor/screen that you can type in a reminder message and display it in the school hallway. There may also be a PA system, which a grad exec member can use to relay a reminder message.

Collect AG Surveys – week three

Although many surveys may have been returned, it may be worthwhile to have a grad exec go to each Grade 12 class and collect any that are hiding out in the bottom of lockers, car backseats, binders, jean pockets, etc. – the more surveys the better!

Tabulate Survey Results & Prepare Survey Report – week three

Once you have the stack of surveys in hand, you can tally the votes and record the information in the survey report. Although we rank the results in order of votes received, we do endeavour to include as many items as possible that receive even a few votes if we have the ability and the funds. We use this information when we start talking to suppliers too. If grads have selected arcade games and have told us which ones they want, that helps us narrow down the selection process with the supplier.

Our sample Survey Report matches our Sample Survey, so you will, of course, need to customize your report to match your survey.

Hopefully your report will provide a clear picture of the type of event your grad class is looking for and will provide the sub-committees with the direction they need to begin to source suppliers, rental companies, entertainment and performers, and everything else that will make your After-Grad unique and unforgettable!

Sample "Survey Report" is available in Appendix – Forms and as a PDF document or as an Excel document at www.safegradevent.com/tools/forms/surveyreport

Distribute Survey Report to AG Committee & Grad Exec – week three

Presenting your Survey Report to your entire AG Committee will give each sub-committee the information they need in order to do their research and make their tentative supplier bookings. Armed with a "wish list" from the grads, sub-committee members can solicit quotes, and then provide those to the finance coordinator who can include these in a "working budget" to present to the next AG Committee meeting.

At this time, you can also distribute the Survey Report to the grad exec. The easiest and most efficient way to distribute the report is by email. It will show them which activities received the highest votes and which theme idea emerged as a winner. It's important for the grads to know that the committee really is designing an event based on their wishes and not the parents' ideas. You may want to attend the next grad exec meeting, answer any outstanding questions and assist with the theme selection if the group still needs some discussion and a final vote. Then you will have what you need for the next AG Committee meeting and you can get to work on helping to develop the theme concept.

Develop Publicity & Print Plan – week three

As early as November may seem, this is a good time to develop a publicity and print plan, assessing your needs to determine what dollars you may need, and create your own "action items" that you can carry out throughout the next 6 or 7 months. Bringing awareness to your local business community will hopefully translate into support for the AG committee's fundraising efforts.

Get in touch with your local TV station and newspaper and let them know about the After-Grad, securing some initial interest/coverage for the ongoing process as well as the actual event. Ask for a designated contact person (an editor or producer or reporter). It is especially important to spread "positive press" about the teens in your community to help ensure that the AG tradition continues, and a local newspaper story or TV spot can go a long way to making that happen. As you move along in the process, give some thought to recognition and how you will highlight the support you have received (including from the media). There are opportunities on the school or society website, newspaper ads, local TV, etc.

To develop a print plan, you will need to review the needs of the various sub-committees so that you can put the dollars aside for the design and production process. It can take time from start to finish but asking now means some initial decisions can be made. In terms of printing needs, a very supportive school administration has meant that we have had few costs associated with this category. Using the school website (a separate AG page works well), and corresponding by email helps reduce printing/mailing costs. If you have an in-school print shop or art department, you may be able to negotiate with them to support your event at a reduced cost, or use your printing project as an "in class" assignment.

If your school offers to provide design or printing services, getting them involved early on makes good sense, and teachers can fit your project into existing programs/ curriculum.

Print needs may include signage, such as an entrance/welcome sign, a large print piece that provides the protocol/entrance guidelines, and room signage listing the various activities and performance times. You may also require casino money, event tickets, and programs, so put a list together so that you can source a print supplier. (If you have to outsource printing, complete a "Quote Sheet" so that your costs can be included in the overall budget that the Finance coordinator creates later on this month.

Note: we combine this budget area with Fundraising and Prizes as it represents such a small percentage of the overall budget.

A sample "Quote Sheet" is available in Appendix – Forms and as a PDF document or as an Excel document at www.safegradevent.com/tools/forms/quotesheet

Create Supplier Contact List – week four

As the sub-committees research and secure suppliers, they will each complete the Quote Sheet which includes all of the suppliers' contact information. Create a data base that includes every supplier, and provides you with a comprehensive list of anyone and everyone associated with the event. This list is especially helpful for the coordinators and sub-committee members who may have dealings with people on the list – everything is captured in one document. I wouldn't want to be without my Supplier Contact List in June!

I record the contacts in alphabetical order by name of supplier but you may also find it useful to sort the list by "description" of service or product, since the names of the suppliers may not be as familiar to all committee members. Because this document is prepared in Excel, it's easy to sort as needed, or to provide a few versions within the one document. And if you don't have access to Excel, you can download the PDF version and create a sheet that works for you.

A sample "Supplier Contact List" is available in Appendix – Forms and as a PDF document or as an Excel document at www.safegradevent.com/tools/forms/suppliercontacts

FINANCE

Create New AG Account/Books – week two

Depending on how involved your school or Parent Council is with the After-Grad, you may need to set up a separate bank account for the event and related funding. You will need to keep accurate records of income and expenses as well as have the ability to write cheques on the account (keep in mind that the total budget may be in the tens of thousands of dollars). If you need to establish society status, and have not started that ball rolling, now is the time to get that up and running, so everything is in place once funds start rolling in. You may want to contact the Canada Revenue Agency or your state or federal tax agency for information on establishing a charitable organization or society.

Develop a Working Budget (a work in progress) – week four

While grad class sizes will vary from coast to coast and school to school, most AG events will include similar components to ours. Our event is based on a group of approximately 200; you will need to adjust your planning to accommodate your group's size. We have developed a budget formula that works with whatever our grads tell us to include each year – we believe this formula will work for any size of group.

Some schools wait several months before setting a budget, watching to see how fundraising efforts are going and how the dollars are looking. Still others, like ours, determine a tentative budget early on, selecting a possible ticket price amount, and using that figure to set a conservative budget, we monitor it throughout the year as fundraising continues and then settle on a final ticket price closer to the event date.

Our budget formula is based on allocating the highest dollar amounts to the most important event components. Since most After-Grads span several hours, many taking place after an already long and emotionally charged day, we have worked hard to make sure that there is high level of comfort at the event, plenty to participate in and lots to see throughout the night. It is vital that the grads feel awake, engaged, and well – without thoughts of leaving early, or heading out to another kind of party. As I said earlier, we truly believe that much of the success that our Parkland After-Grad enjoys each year is due to the fact that we concentrate our efforts on keeping everyone completely entertained!

In developing your working budget, you will need to take into account all sources of income and try to anticipate many or all of the expenses. It is best to be conservative with the budget, for a couple of reasons. One is that costs change as you move along from one year into the next and you may alter the event content. There needs to be money available for those changes or unforeseen expenses. As well, since the event is primarily funded by ticket sales and fundraising efforts, it can be difficult to guess seven months out, how much money you will have in the end. For most groups, this event is parent sponsored and run and not a school run event, so there may be *no* available funding from any school budget – you cannot owe money in the end. Fortunately, there are many fundraising and income opportunities available, so it is possible to raise quite a bit of money in support of an AG event, and to lower the price of the ticket so that everyone can afford to attend. Private donations, local councils, gaming funds, PAC donations and ticket sales can more than cover the cost of the event, especially if the grads put a plan together early on in the school year.

With many or all of the supplier quotes now in hand, you can start to input the information from the various sub-committee quote sheets and determine where your event is under and over budget. It's great to be able to do this in November, because you still have lots of time for fundraising and to make decisions about what you can afford to include in the event. By working with the highest number of survey votes for particular components, you can be sure to include the grads' "must-dos" in the budget and still leave room to contemplate other ideas if the funds become available further along in the process. And, if the sub-committees have tentatively booked the suppliers, those companies or individuals will usually hold your date, until they receive another request, and at that time, the AG committee can make a decision as to whether or not to confirm a particular component.

If this is your first year and you are starting out with no school funding, you may be starting with a zero budget, as we did back in 2005. Each year we develop a very conservative working budget based on a maximum ticket price and an attendance formula. We assume that the majority of tickets are paid for by parents, not by students so we ask parents for a price point they can live with, and then use the approved maximum as our starting ticket price. We then fundraise throughout the year in order to lower the final AG ticket price while securing enough money for us to operate the event.

To determine the remaining budget amount, we use the following formula:

- ✓ We determine a guest count, starting with the total number of Grade 12 students in the grad class
- ✓ We reduce it by 5% to represent those that that might not graduate
- ✓ We further reduce that total by another 5% for those who might not attend (we are optimistic, and expect 95% attendance). "Start out the way you intend to continue" is one of my mottos, so we decide we are going to have a full house!
- ✓ We add another 10% to represent guests (we permit grads to bring guests from other grades and other local high schools)
- ✓ Our grad class of 200 becomes a guest count of 200 − 10 = 190 − 9 = 181 + 18 = 199. Our numbers have usually turned out to be very close to our estimates, and we have had a full house each year.

With your two starting figures (we assigned a $90.00 maximum ticket price for 2010), you can create a working budget total, and then begin to break it down by budget/sub-committee category. Your intent is that along the way, you will be able to add to your total funds and/or reduce the ticket price with fundraising and donated dollars. Our grads opted for a higher ticket price with more fundraising dollars going to prizes. Many schools, however, aim for a ticket price of $50.00 or less which makes the event much more affordable for all.

Final pricing decisions can be made later on – for now you need to determine a starting point to determine what you can afford to include in the event. When breaking out our budget we make some assumptions as to how much money should be allocated to each area or category, based on their level of importance to the event. With my experience as an event planner and the mother of three teenagers to guide me, I know that once they have been "wowed" by the decor, they are looking for entertainment, games, contests and food. Six to seven hours is a long time in which to entertain a group of any size, especially a group of teens!

When drafting a budget, I record the "hard costs" first, those that won't or can't change – items such as the venue rental, security, transportation, etc. – these have to be included so they go in early on and often won't change. Costs such as live entertainment or games rentals are more a matter of preference (based on the survey results) and costs will fluctuate depending on what is chosen. So, with a number of entertainment options available and the grad survey selection information, we base our decisions on the level of impact each idea will make, and the most we can provide with our funds.

As an example, each year we have included caricature artists, because we love the idea of the grads having something to take away with them to remember the event. We recognize that one won't be enough for a group our size, so we budget for one with the hope that later on, we may find additional funds and add a second artist – which we have done each year. The budget is constantly moving and changing because you are soliciting quotes and securing suppliers almost eight months before the actual event, and costs can increase from year to year. Remember to build some "just in case" funds into your budget too, just in case costs increase or you incur added expenses that you can't foresee. Hopefully, when all is said and done, and the bills have all been paid, you will end up with a small balance to carry over to the next graduating class, just as we have each year since the beginning.

The sample budget we show in our template is similar to our 2010 budget and shows the various categories to which we allocated our funds. We use similar categories as suggested for each sub-committee. Keep in mind that some sub-committees may be responsible for more than one budget area and others may have little or no budget allocated such as Fundraising & Prizes, an area where more dollars come in than go out (we combine the

Communications & Publicity budget with Fundraising & Prizes as it represents such a small percentage of the overall budget). Remember, the more fundraising dollars you can include in your "income" column, the lower the ticket price becomes.

The sample "Budget" is available in Appendix – Forms and as a PDF document or as an Excel document at www.safegradevent.com/tools/forms/budget

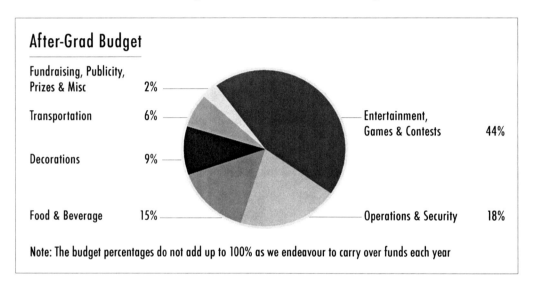

 **VOLUNTEER**

Create Volunteer Data Base – week three

Hopefully by now you have been able to collect many more parent names and email addresses and can continue to build on the data base you began in September/October to use throughout the year. This list will be very useful when it comes time to correspond with your large group of event volunteers. If you also have a "grad" list, you can cross reference to determine which parents are missing, and you can use this time to get that contact information before things really heat up in the New Year.

In addition to grad parents, there are other sources of volunteers within the school and local community. Don't forget about grade 9 to 11 parents who have future grads, grandparents, service organizations who may have programs with a "volunteer" mandate, and youth pastors. You are not alone – there is lots of support out there!

 ## TRANSPORTATION, OPERATIONS, & SAFETY

Venue Walk Through – week one

If you participated in a venue walk through in October, you may not feel the need to do another, but it can be very helpful to now look at the venue with an eye to security, safety and wellness.

Visit the venue and check out all of the access points, including ramps for supplier installations and wheelchair accessibility; be aware of exit points – these will need to be manned during the event, since exit doors will be unlocked (you must have emergency and evacuation exits available at all times) If your event includes outdoor games or event space, you will need to determine your "secured perimeter" area so you can solicit quotes for perimeter fencing. This is also a good time to establish designated entry and exit points for the event; remember to allow enough room for line-ups, security procedures, etc. Check out the parking facilities, as well as where buses/cars can load/unload.

Have a look at the washroom facilities, and establish a location for your Wellness Room (where the wellness team will "live" during the event, possibly with volunteers and suppliers). The more you do now to cover off on the safety and security of the event, the more time and effort you can devote to the fun.

Record notes during your walk through so you can pass these on to the AG sub-committees and also the security firm and/or police prior to the event. And be sure to ask your security team representative to plan for a "sweep" of the entire venue prior to your group's arrival so you can be sure that no one has stashed anything during the daytime hours, to be used later at the event. Our security team does a complete sweep about 30 minutes prior to our guests' arrival each year.

Source and Secure Suppliers – week four

With the survey report in hand, your sub-committee can now start sourcing suppliers. Try to source locally where possible, for two reasons. It's great to support local business (some of whom may become sponsors), and you can reduce costs by not paying extra travel or accommodation for out-of-town suppliers. Ask your venue representative for recommended suppliers too because they will have worked with many of the same suppliers you are contacting and can make recommendations as well as warn you off those they don't recommend. Be sure to explain to suppliers what you are trying to achieve with a safe dry all-night event. This may help secure their participation and may even lead to discounts, as many having had their own children graduate or be graduating in coming years will "buy" in to the concept.

Use email to contact suppliers and to confirm their involvement. It provides an ongoing means of contact throughout the next few months, as well as an important paper trail, providing confirmation and rates in writing. Later on it will serve as a quick and easy way to provide purchase orders, event schedules and maps. Remember to include as much contact information as possible on your Quote Sheet, as this information will be added to a Supplier Contact List. For those suppliers willing to provide firm pricing, you may need to review contracts and request deposits in order to hold the quote and secure their services. We use our carryover funds from the previous year for these deposits; you may also be able to request funding through your PAC at this time, if you have no available event funds. And, lastly, ask lots of questions – I have included a list of supplier questions you can ask, along with a list of a few suppliers (available on the website) with whom we have had success with over the past five years – they have supported us every step of the way.

TRANSPORTATION – Unless grads and guests are arriving to the event on their own, moving them to and from the event venue is a cost that has to be incurred (a hard cost), which makes this a good cost to determine early on. If it takes more than 5 to 7% of the total budget, you can always adjust the budget in other areas where there is more flexibility, in areas that are not as vital to the event's success or in "soft cost" areas such as decorating and entertainment, where you can negotiate what you spend.

There are a number of ways in which to transport guests to an AG venue, and depending on what is going on prior to this event, parents and other volunteer drivers may be the least expensive way to move the group, or buses may turn out to be the best option. For our event, our group arrives from their school-sponsored dinner/dance at an out of town location, so parent drivers are not readily available. We use buses as they are the most cost effective and efficient way to move our group of 200 grads and guests.

We charter double-decker buses because they are a fun "Victoria" way to arrive and can hold up to 70 guests at one time, many of whom have never been on a double-decker. For the return transfer home, we use school buses or full-sized motorcoaches as this is the most cost effective way to move such a large group. Always mention the type of event; some suppliers will give discounts for school groups and not-for-profit events, and some will believe in and want to support your "safe dry" event. Bus suppliers may want to know about a "staging" area, where buses can wait until it's time to load them with guests, and they may have access questions about the width of entrances/exits, and will want to know if you want the entire group to arrive together or if you prefer a staggered arrival. We prefer a staggered arrival as the security line-up can be slow, and it allows for better control with one or two buses at a time, vs. all four for example. Answers to your bus supplier questions can be provided by the venue or your sub-committee chair who secured the venue. I always plan on a cash gratuity for our bus drivers, so that may need to be added into your budget amount.

OPERATIONS – Operations costs are also considered hard costs, so again, determining these early on gives you a much better idea of your working budget. These costs include the venue rental which may include several additional components. It may include staffing, janitorial services, security services and much more. Depending on the venue, some may even include decor items so always check your contract carefully to see what is/isn't included and to see what other products and services may be available for purchase/rent. (You will have determined this in your venue walk through, when you asked all those questions). We have been fortunate in that our venue rental has always included some overnight staffing, janitorial services, a private security firm and the mandatory SOCAN (music licensing) fees for any entertainment. We have also had access to tables and chairs, some soft furnishings such as couches and some plants and buffet tables. As you have already secured the venue, you should already know most of the costs for this budget area and will be ready to input these into your Quote Sheet.

SAFETY AND SECURITY – Safety and security are paramount to a "safe" grad and it's important you put systems in place and take the necessary steps to provide a secure environment. Having done a venue walk through, you should now be familiar with the layout including all access points, and should be able to put a plan in place, along with the support of your venue representative to ensure a safe event.

Your "safety plan" will include all members of your security team, which may consist of a professional security firm, along with additional parent volunteers. As security is a vital component of your event, ask the venue, your local police department, or a local event planning company for a supplier recommendation.

You may also want to include a paid police presence, or at least register the event with your local police department. Police officers add a level of comfort to the event as well as send a clear message that the event will be "dry and safe" as advertised (some events include police officers with breathalyzers at the entrance doors). Our school police liaison officer has always been a welcome addition to our event, especially as he already has a relationship with the school administration and many if not all of the graduates. Your "safety" plan may start at the registration area, with the cost of guest ID wristbands (many event/liability insurance companies require an identification process) to ensure that attendance has been paid for and recorded. These can be sourced online, and are generally an inexpensive budget item.

Included in this area of safety and security is the "change of clothes." Grads and guests arriving to the After-Grad are usually dressed up in beautiful suits, gowns, and in some cases, like our sons, kilts. Most will want to change into something more comfortable long before 5 or 6 am, so a change of clothes needs to be available. And that change of clothes needs to be checked just like anything else brought into the event. There are a number of systems used by groups. Some have clothes dropped off a few days prior to the event to a parent group who does the actual security check before delivering them to the venue ahead of the event – labelled and sorted, ready for pickup in the Coat Check area. Others schools have the grads/guests bring their own change of clothes with them to the event. At Parkland, we have the clothes dropped off to the venue earlier that same day, ready to go through the security check with them when they arrive to the event. Still others prefer to ask the grads to change immediately after the dinner/dance so they are already in their comfortable clothing when they arrive to the event.

Also included in this area are all other "operational" and "wellness" costs. As the event may involve outside work or activities, operational costs may include radio rentals, flashlights, high-visibility security vests for outside volunteers, sleeping mats/linens, coat check supplies, volunteer crew needs, and washroom amenities.

Our "wellness team" includes a combination of doctors, nurses, paramedics, firefighters/first responders and counsellors. We have been fortunate each year to have filled these roles with volunteer parents from within our grad class, which has greatly reduced our costs in this area. If no volunteers are available, there are professional organizations you can contact that can provide volunteer or paid services.

If the venue or school does not provide a first aid kit, you may need to purchase one for the event, along with any "wellness" or "comfort" supplies you want to provide. Over the years, our supply list has included over-the-counter headache and stomach upset remedies, earplugs, eye masks, feminine hygiene products, toothpaste and toothbrushes, mouthwash and contact lens solutions – things that are used to refresh after a long grad day and/or that grads may have forgotten to bring along. If you are able to get any of these items donated, it will reduce your costs in this area. And remember, after the event, when storing for next year's event, you must safely and responsibly discard any items that will expire before next year's event date.

And finally, a secure coat check area will provide an additional level of safety for any guest valuables that require storage, including cell phones, cameras, etc. If your venue is a recreation/leisure centre, you may have access to individual lockers to keep items safe during the event.

The sample "Supplier Questions" sheet is available in Appendix – Forms and as a PDF document or as a Word document at www.safegradevent.com/tools/form/supplierquestions

Our 2010 sample budget includes:
- ✓ the buses we use to transfer our grads from the dinner/dance location to the AG location,
- ✓ the buses we use to transfer our grads from the AG location back to our local shopping centre in town, where awaiting parent drivers can pick up their grads,
- ✓ the cost of the venue rental, janitorial services, security firm, SOCAN entertainment licensing fees, and
- ✓ the ID wristbands, wellness room supplies, first aid kit, coat check supplies, volunteer crew needs including flashlights and earplugs (nightclub), and washroom amenities.

Secure Wellness and Security Team – week four

Having sourced a professional security firm along with a police presence to ensure grad safety and security, you may also want create a sense of "wellness" at the event, which includes a separate room for guests who need to relax, rest, just take a break from the activities. Lights are dim, while mats and bedding provide a resting place. As you can imagine, with such a long and emotional day, there are guests who are tired, may have headaches, have forgotten to eat or stay hydrated, or just need some support or comfort (boyfriend/girlfriend breakups are the number one support issue). For those guests who may require medication, they can spend time in the Wellness Room where there is supervision, and assistance if needed, all in a somewhat private setting.

There will be time before the event to meet and organize your wellness team, but for now you can concentrate on building your team with the names of available individuals. St. John Ambulance is a worldwide organization that is dedicated to meeting local community needs and may be a great resource for this type of event. Search the web for your local chapter.

During the event, most of our wellness team remains in the Wellness Room (at least one doctor and one nurse) so they are available immediately should an emergency situation arise. Other team members may roam the event to keep a watchful eye and to handle onsite situations that may not require additional assistance or services in the Wellness Room. We encourage our captive doctors and nurses to bring laptops and books/magazines along for the night, as we hope it's a very "uneventful" event – no emergencies, no issues, no patients.

With regards to medical treatment onsite, our grad/guest agreements request information on any medical/food issues, concerns or requirements. This information is kept confidential and is provided only to the wellness team (doctor, nurse, paramedic and police officer) onsite so that they can assist if needed or to provide valuable information in the case of an emergency, such as a food allergy or immediate need for medication.

In April, when the AG Binder is created, these agreements will be filed alphabetically and can be referred to by the wellness team in cases where they need to make an informed decision on the grad/guest's behalf.

Develop Quote Sheet – week four

For this budget area, I try to keep my percentages within 5 to 7% for transportation and approximately 20% for operations, safety & security. Now that you have all of your supplier quotes in hand, it's time to plug them into a Quote Sheet and then you can forward that sheet to the finance coordinator to build into the overall budget. Once every sub-committee has handed in their quote sheets, you will have a very good idea of the overall budget and the funds you will need to raise in order to operate the event. Having all of the numbers in front of you will also help you make decisions about where to cut costs.

A sample "Quote Sheet" is available in Appendix – Forms and as a PDF document or as an Excel document at www.safegradevent.com/tools/forms/quotesheet

DECORATING, FOOD & BEVERAGE

Research and Select Food & Beverage (F&B) Provider – week two

Food and beverage [F&B] is a large component of any event, especially one which includes a large group of teens – or "eating machines" as they are known in my house. There is room for flexibility in this area though, as you will have many options in terms of what to include. The timing of your event and the day's earlier events will also impact your F&B decisions. Because our event follows the school-sponsored dinner/dance, we don't need to provide a great deal of food early on. We follow a similar plan each year, and change it according to the survey results. If your group is arriving directly from home, many hours past the dinner hour, your F&B needs will differ.

The source of food can also vary. Our After-Grad has been held each year on our local university campus where they provide onsite catering so our work in this area has been simplified, using the venue's menus. Some groups have local grocery stores and restaurants provide food, and still others bring in caterers, or use in-house cafeterias. For us, because the venue staff are responsible for setting the buffets and distributing the food items, we don't incur additional staffing charges besides what is built into the menu pricing. A supplier/caterer may charge for onsite staff, and may have to include some rentals, if items such as serving pieces, plates, etc., are not available from the venue. The caterer will include all of these charges in your quote, so you will know upfront what all of the costs will be.

Whatever direction you select, the F&B providers you contact will provide you with suggested menus and quantities for your group size, and will include in a detailed and complete quote any rentals and/or staff they will require that night. Ask about being "charged on consumption" or charged for only what is consumed, wherever possible, rather than providing a guarantee of amounts. For example, we purchase our coffee based on consumption so we only pay for what the guests actually drink, rather than having to guess on quantities – this also reduces waste.

Keep in mind that you may want to include some alternative F&B options such as hot dogs, popcorn, and cotton candy machines. These can be rented from party rental suppliers (caterers will often have suggested contacts).

Working with caterers, restaurants or local grocers can be a real pleasure; they are experts in the food business, and are usually self-sufficient onsite so you can concentrate on other areas of concern during the event, knowing they are taking care of this very important event component.

I have included a sample list of questions along with the information about the event that you will need to have on hand when speaking to or meeting with a food and beverage provider/supplier.

"Food Provider Questions" is available in Appendix – Forms and as a PDF document or as a Word document at www.safegradevent.com/tools/forms/foodproviderquestions

Source and Secure Suppliers – week four

With the survey report in hand, your sub-committee can now start sourcing suppliers. As mentioned previously, try to source locally where possible, for two reasons – it's great to support local business (some of whom may become sponsors), and you can reduce costs by not paying extra travel or accommodation for out-of-town suppliers. Ask your venue representative for recommended suppliers because they will have worked with many of the same suppliers you are contacting and can make recommendations as well as subtly warn you off those they don't recommend. Be sure to explain to a potential supplier what you are trying to achieve with a safe dry all-night event. It may lead to discounts, as many small business owners have kids themselves and will support your ideals.

Even if you make phone calls or talk in person, it is recommended that you use email to contact suppliers to confirm their involvement. Emailing provides an ongoing means of contact throughout the next few months, as well as an important paper trail, providing confirmation and rates in writing. Later on it will serve as a quick-and-easy way to provide purchase orders, event schedules and maps. Remember to include as much contact information as possible on your Quote Sheet, as this information will be added to a Supplier Contact List. For those suppliers willing to provide firm pricing, you may need to review contracts and pay a deposit in order to hold the quote and secure their services. We use our carryover funds from the previous year for these deposits; you may also be able to request funding through your PAC at this time if you have no available event funds. And lastly, ask lots of questions – I have included a list of supplier questions plus contact information on some of the suppliers (available on the website) with whom we have had success over the past five years.

Items that fall into this budget area are considered "soft costs" as it's really up to your sub-committee how much you want to spend and how elaborate you want to get. Now that you have a sense of who might be providing the food and beverage for your event, it's time to research some decorating and party rental suppliers. As mentioned previously, while we try to incorporate the theme into our event in as many ways as possible, decorating always takes a back seat to entertainment. Your guests won't remember too much of what they *see* once they have been onsite for a while; they will however be looking for lots to *do* and *experience* in their many hours at the event, and will be looking to make memories! Decorating is such a fun part of the event, but a word of advice: it's really easy to get carried away with all the beautiful and magical set pieces and decor items that are available, so keep your budget in mind and practice saying "no" to that fabulous 10-foot Eiffel Tower that would look great in the nightclub!

The decorating component includes the overall look of the event space right down to the table decor and novelty items handed out to grads and guests. Event and party rental companies will have the bigger pieces including the outdoor decor items such as carpet, stanchions, benches, trees and set pieces, as well as table linens, skirting and table/buffet centrepieces. Local theatre companies are a good source for larger set pieces also, as are school theatre groups and local service organizations, as they often will loan free of charge or for a nominal fee. Florists can also provide trees, table centres and additional themed pieces. Take into consideration whether it is more cost effective and/or better for the environment to rent or buy decorating items. Renting means you won't have to store it, find additional or future uses, and best of all, it won't end up later in a landfill. Since themes tend to change from year to year, themed items are often better rental options. Buying, if you have storage, can be a very cost effective option, especially for items that you will use from year to year, such as some games (foosball, air hockey), tea lights, etc. You may only be working on this year's committee, but the After-Grad will continue long after you have left your school, so think "big picture" about items you are certain will be used annually.

Costumes, novelty items and giveaways also fall within this budget. Each year, we ask our parent volunteers and entertainers to wear something to suit the theme. We also add some rental costumes that are themed, including our mermaid and pirates for our 2010 tropical theme. We add in novelty items that we distribute on the bus seats as a surprise, along with flashing body pins for volunteers and beach balls and glow sticks for the nightclub. Many of these items are very inexpensive and we buy them online each year which saves a great deal of money. These items make a big difference to the event and can fill a room with "walking decor" for very little money, while providing a souvenir of the event. Need some more convincing? Consider:

- ✓ They represent what the event is – fun, celebratory, exciting and the theme
- ✓ They represent a small % of the budget and really add to the "look" of the event
- ✓ They make a big impact, at a small price
- ✓ The guests love them! When they board the bus, they actually scream, then trade items, and when they arrive at the venue, they really arrive!

- ✓ They add texture, colour, and dimension to the guest and to the room
- ✓ Each year we find less than 5 items left at the venue and we donate any extras or leftovers to a local childcare centre, drama school or dance studio
- ✓ They make a great, fun souvenir of a memorable night
- ✓ They look great in pictures
- ✓ They encourage those who might be shy or conservative to join in, be part of the group and feel a sense of belonging

The example "Supplier Questions" sheet is available in Appendix – Forms and as a PDF document or as a Word document at www.safegradevent.com/tools/forms/supplierquestions

Our 2010 sample budget includes:

- ✓ Outdoor entrance decor – flashing marquee sign, red carpet and stanchions, lighting, and bus novelties for the transfer to the event
- ✓ Indoor room and table decor – table linens and skirting, buffet and table centrepieces, toys including flashing pins, beach balls and glow sticks for the nightclub, theme props and plants, and volunteer costumes
- ✓ All passed food and buffet food items – finger foods, fresh fruit, dessert items
- ✓ Fresh 'to order' pizza vendor, hot dog machine rental and all supplies, popcorn machine rental and all supplies
- ✓ All beverages including welcome mocktails, bottled water, hot coffee, soft drinks/juices

Develop Quote Sheet – week four

For this budget area, I aim to keep my percentages within 10% for decor and 15% for food & beverage. Now that you have all of your supplier quotes in hand, it's time to plug them into a Quote Sheet and then you can forward that sheet to the finance coordinator to build into the overall budget. Once every sub-committee has handed in their Quote Sheets, you will have a very good idea of the overall budget and the funds you will need to raise in order to operate the event. Having all of the numbers in front of you will also help you make decisions about where to cut costs.

The sample "Quote Sheet" is available in Appendix – Forms and as a PDF document or as an Excel document at www.safegradevent.com/tools/forms/quotesheet

ENTERTAINMENT, GAMES & CONTESTS

Source & Secure Suppliers – week four

With the survey report in hand, your sub-committee can now start sourcing suppliers. As we've mentioned previously, sourcing locally not only cuts extra travel and accommodation costs of out-of-town providers, but helps our local small business economy – some of whom have children recently graduated or soon to be.

By using email to contact suppliers and to confirm their involvement, you will have an ongoing means of contact throughout the next few months, as well as an important paper trail, providing confirmation and rates in writing. Having all this information "online" makes it easier to share with other committee members. Gather as much contact information as possible on your Quote Sheet, as this information will be added into a Supplier Contact List. For those suppliers willing to provide firm pricing, you may need to review contracts and pay a deposit to guarantee prices and reserve their services. We use our carryover funds from the previous year for these deposits; if you have no available event funds, you may be able to request funding through your PAC.

Entertainment is, by far, the largest allocation of funds for the entire budget, and the single most important component of the event. I truly believe that the choice and number of entertainment options provided is directly linked to the success or failure of any After-Grad. It is absolutely vital that everyone is thoroughly "entertained."

During the past five years, our survey results have differed only slightly each year. This has meant that we have been able to book some of the same entertainers for several years in a row. And in checking with other schools and Dry Grad groups, most teens want the same things – lots of interactive entertainment, live performances, and the latest in electronic fun! Researching sources of entertainment can be challenging, as you may not have an opportunity to see/hear your performers prior to your event. My advice is that you get plenty of recommendations – ask your parent community, your venue, your school and others for names and review video footage, check out internet links so you know what you are getting when you sign a contract. And, ask questions – I have included a list of performer/entertainer questions you can ask along with a list of some of the performers (available on the website) with whom we have had success over the past five years – they have supported us every step of the way and have provided countless hours of outstanding entertainment.

Keep in mind that some performers are booked up to two years in advance, and that most graduation events are booked for June, just like yours, so it makes sense to get in touch now, to check availability, costs, and then tentatively book if possible. Many will "pencil" you in and then as you move along and determine what funds are available, you can start to secure those that you want to confirm. Many will also offer you first refusal, giving you an opportunity to firm up by signing a contract and/or providing a deposit if someone else inquires for the same date. By the time that happens, you may have a firm working budget, so don't be afraid to make a booking now to ensure your grads won't be disappointed later on. Try to hold off on signing contracts and making deposits if possible, but know that you will need to provide these along with agreements and floor plans later on. For now, it's important to place holds and start building your entertainment Quote Sheet.

When corresponding with performers and entertainers, ask them if they might be able to incorporate the theme. For a tropical theme, a caricature artist can include palm trees, a sun and a parrot in the background. A tattoo artist can offer themed tattoo designs, and a DJ can play tropical tunes.

When it comes to live performances and roaming entertainers, there are options galore! Over the years our events have included DJs, karaoke, local rock bands, magicians, jugglers, fortune tellers, hypnotists, comedians, tattoo artists, caricaturists, actors, dancers, videographers, photographers, photo booths, and interactive games and contests. As well as the performance fees, you will also be responsible for entertainment licensing or SOCAN fees in Canada (contact ASCAP in the US) if you are including music in your event. Your venue may collect these on your behalf, but the fees will need to be included in your budget.

Our static entertainment or games have included casino games such as blackjack and poker, movies, digital photo loops, video games such as *XBOX 360, Rock Band,* and *Nintendo Wii*, arcade games such as *Pac-Man* and pinball, foosball, air hockey, bingo, billiards, souvenir T-shirts, and TV sports and music programs.

Contests are fun too, and get the body moving (this can be a welcome addition at 2 am when guests are tired and bodies are weary). Our 2010 tropical theme included a beach relay, a hula hoop contest, a limbo competition and a competitive game of *TWISTER*.

If your AG event is held at a local recreation or leisure centre you may have the added benefit of swimming pools, arenas, tennis and squash courts, and event rooms. You may also include "outside" spaces and may be able to accommodate inflatables (sumo wrestling, bungee run), or volleyball on a parking lot – all which can add an entirely different dimension of fun and entertainment.

Based on your entertainment selections, you may require audio visual products or services. Your school is a great resource for screens, monitors, laptops, projectors, etc., so try to borrow as much as you can, because AV costs may be high, especially as they will include some installation/technical labour along with delivery and return/pickup. If you have a technically-minded volunteer, they can set up electronic and video games which may save you time and money as the AV supplier doesn't have to stay onsite too long.

I recommend that you have the volunteer sub-committee assign a volunteer to "handle" your entertainers and performers, making sure that they get their breaks, are fed and watered, and payments issued – it is good to provide the volunteer sub-committee as much information as possible about your entertainer/performer needs.

The sample "Performer Questions" sheet is available in Appendix – Forms and as a PDF document or as a Word document at www.safegradevent.com/tools/forms/performer questions

Our 2010 sample budget included:

- ✓ Casino game rentals (blackjack, poker, wheel, bingo) – no money used in this casino – guests play to build wealth to win a prize later in the prize draw
- ✓ Static game rentals including video games (*XBOX 360, Nintendo Wii, DDR, Rock Band*), foosball, air hockey and a pool table
- ✓ Standalone arcade games such as pinball and *Pac Man*, a photo booth, and souvenir signed T-shirts
- ✓ Contest pieces including rentals, game props, etc.
- ✓ All live performances – caricaturists, airbrush tattoo artists (don't worry, they are temporary, lasting about three weeks), magicians, karaoke host, DJ, hypnotist/comedian, bands

Develop Quote Sheet – week four

For this budget area, I try to keep my percentages within 45 to 50% for all entertainment including live performances, static games and interactive contest. Now that you have all of your supplier quotes in hand, it's time to plug them into a Quote Sheet and then you can forward that sheet to the finance coordinator to build into the overall budget. Once every committee has handed in their Quote Sheets, you will have a very good idea of the overall budget and the funds you will need to raise in order to operate the event. Having all of the numbers in front of you will also help you make decisions about where to cut costs.

A sample "Quote Sheet" is available in Appendix – Forms and as a PDF document or as an Excel document at www.safegradevent.com/tools/forms/quotesheet

 ## FUNDRAISING & PRIZES

Research Fundraising Opportunities and Develop Initial Plan – week three

Before you start brainstorming fundraising ideas, make sure that you have your paperwork in order. In order to run a raffle, provide donor receipts, sell event tickets, etc., you must have the required licenses and permits in order. Depending on whether your are operating through your school, your Parent Council or as a separate non-profit group or society, you may already have the systems in place, but always check with local government agencies/authorities as to current gaming and licensing requirements.

As you consider all of the opportunities for raising awareness, dollars and donations, keep in mind that this is a wonderful opportunity to garner community support. There will be community members who are able to donate time, money, space, food, etc., so be sure to reach out to the community and include them whenever possible. Keep in mind that donors and sponsors sometimes require months of advance notice in order to prepare and deliver their donations and services, and some budgets are set early on for the entire fiscal year so the earlier you request, the better. Large companies and corporations often require applications for funding be submitted long before the event, and some have a lengthy approval process so although the event is still months away, November is not too soon to get started.

In terms of fundraising there is no shortage of great ideas. The internet is one amazing resource. Search under "school fundraisers" or "fundraising ideas" and you will be inundated with suggestions. Your school may already have participated in some very successful fundraisers, so talk to your Parent Council and grad parents. Don't forget other options that may include private donations, local town/municipality councils, lottery/gaming funds, local school boards, PAC donations, and the previous year's event's profits/carryover.

Some of the most successful AG fundraisers have included:
- ✓ Grad Fashion Show, with silent auction, and Dessert Café
- ✓ Bottle drives, car washes, bake sales, themed lunches, outdoor movie showings
- ✓ Grocery, coffee, books, gas reward or points programs
- ✓ Seasonal plants/flowers, chocolates, books/magazines, sales programs
- ✓ Local business proceeds – a percentage of sales dedicated to the After-Grad
- ✓ Dances, pub nights, concerts, hockey games, golf tournaments
- ✓ Gourmet baskets, home product parties, clothing drives
- ✓ Liquor stores – some will allow an in-store collection program for dry After-Grads
- ✓ Grad Raffle – include a local business as the source for the raffle prizes and have all grads sell tickets as well as sell within the community

Local businesses and community organizations are your best source of prize dollars and donations. Each year our grads make their way out into the community to talk to local business owners and professionals to solicit funds for tuitions and bursaries as well as prizes for the AG prize draw. In addition, each year our school's Parent Council has secured a gaming license in order to run our very successful grad raffle. While prizes are not necessary, they can prove to be a powerful draw for AG participation, and were one of the incentives we offered at our first ever After-Grad. In 2010, our grads raised over $10,000 in their raffle, which meant every grad took home a prize from the event, and some lucky guests took some amazing computers, iPhones, and TVs to their college and university dorms in September. Many AG events give away a car as the grand prize (our school did this at our first event in 2006).

As you work on your fundraising campaign and determine dates for opportunities, remember to add these into your "Action Items" for each month.

Create a Funding & Prizes Contact List – week three

As you make your initial contacts, create a contact list for reference and for follow-up later on in the year. You can use the Supplier Contact List as a template, making any necessary adjustments.

The sample "Supplier Contact List" is available in Appendix – Forms and as a PDF document or as a Word document at www.safegradeevent.com/tools/forms/suppliercontact

Source and Secure Suppliers – week four

With the survey report in hand, your sub-committee can now start sourcing suppliers/donors. Try to source local donors where possible for all donations. The more fundraising dollars you raise, the fewer budget funds you will need to use for prizes. You may find that you won't have much to add into the budget, since you will be soliciting funds rather than spending them, so you may have few expenses in this area. Be sure to explain to suppliers/donors what you are trying to achieve with a safe dry all-night event.

Use email to contact suppliers/donors and to confirm their involvement as this provides an ongoing means of contact throughout the next few months, as well as an important paper trail, providing confirmation in writing. Remember to secure as much contact information as possible as this information will be added to a Supplier Contact List.

An initial blanket email to all of the suppliers/donors you are interested in can save time – include information about dry, safe, After-Grad events , some event details that you know – date, event timing, venue location, group size, theme, etc. Once drafted, these letters can be forwarded to the Communications & Publicity Coordinator for distribution and follow up in January.

A sample "Prize/Donation Solicitation" letter is available in Appendix – Forms and as a PDF document or as a Word document at www.safegradevent.com/tools/forms/prizesolicitation

A sample "Tuition Solicitation Letter" is available in Appendix – Forms and as a PDF document or as a Word document at www.safegradevent.com/tools/forms/tuitionsolicitation

Our 2010 sample budget includes:

- ✓ "miscellaneous" money
- ✓ newspaper Thank-You ad for prize sponsors/donors

Develop Quote Sheet – week four

For this budget area, which includes 'publicity' too, I try to keep my percentages within 5 to 10% of the overall budget. If you can secure donations in this area, it will save money. If you have any supplier/donor quotes in hand, plug them into a Quote Sheet for the finance coordinator to incorporate into the overall budget. (The Communications and Publicity sub-committee will have print costs available for this budget area.) Once every sub-committee has handed in their Quote Sheets, you will have a very good idea of the overall budget and the funds you will need to raise in order to operate the event, and any cost-cutting required. You may not have any costs associated with this area as you are hopefully working with donations rather than expenses.

A sample "Quote Sheet" is available in Appendix – Forms and as a PDF document or as an Excel document at www.safegradevent.com/tools/forms/quotesheet

AG Committee Meeting – week four

At this meeting, it may make sense to use this time and the group's collective heads to further develop the theme concept. If the survey results showed two themes close in votes, consider putting some thoughts together on both, and then presenting them to the grad executive. It may provide a clearer vision of what each theme might look like.

"Graduation is a major moment for us and an event that most definitely stands out in our lives. It is something many of us would not only like to remember but enjoy as much as possible. When alcohol is thrown into the equation it opens up the possibility for over-consumption and the many negative effects that may come with it. Why not soak up every moment you can rather than impair your experience. It is truly an experience I'll never forget. They are memories I wouldn't trade in for the world."

— Patrick, graduate

DECEMBER

As mentioned earlier, December is a very busy month, both for school and family so we usually put our AG work aside until January. For the same reasons and because we generally enjoy a 2-week school break this month, we don't hold a December AG meeting.

It may be very different where you live, so if you have the time, use this month to complete any outstanding action items from earlier on. Of course, if you have time and want to meet as a group, why not get together and discuss your event status and make a plan for January?

DECEMBER – ACTION ITEMS

Week	Chair	Communications & Publicity Co-ordinator	Finances Co-ordinator	Volunteer Committee	Transportation, Operations & Safety Committee	Decorating, Food & Beverage Committee	Entertainment, Games & Contests Committee	Fundraising & Prizes Committee
Week 1								
Week 2								
Week 3								
Week 4								

Sample "Action Items – December" is available as a PDF document or Excel document at www.safegradevent.com/tools/forms/actionitemsdecember

"You steered the ship and put in those countless hours of prep and planning, and thought of every single tiny detail. I am so glad that you have turned all your hard work into a book so this can be duplicated year after year now."

— Shevaun, parent volunteer

JANUARY

January represents the start of a new year and for the After-Grad; it means you have about 5 or 6 months until the big event! This month is not quite as busy as some, so you have time to review what's been accomplished and to work on any outstanding action items that didn't get completed before the December break.

JANUARY – ACTION ITEMS

Week	Chair	Communications & Publicity Co-ordinator	Finances Co-ordinator	Volunteer Committee	Transportation, Operations & Safety Committee	Decorating, Food & Beverage Committee	Entertainment, Games & Contests Committee	Fundraising & Prizes Committee
Week 1								
Week 2		Distribute Solicitation Letters		Set Volunteer Information Meeting & Training Date for May				
Week 3								
Week 4	AG Committee Meeting	AG Committee Meeting	AG Committee Meeting	AG Committee Meeting	AG Committee Meeting	AG Committee Meeting	AG Committee Meeting	AG Committee Meeting

Sample "Action Items – January" is available as a PDF document or Excel document at www.safegradevent.com/tools/forms/actionitemsjanuary

COMMUNICATIONS & PUBLICITY

Distribute Solicitation Letters – week two

The fundraising sub-committee may have a list of contacts and solicitation draft letters for you to work with this month, as they reach out into the community to create awareness and solicit support, fundraising dollars and prize donations. Sending these out early in the year gives local businesses time to consider the requests and see how they fit within their budget.

 # VOLUNTEER

Set Volunteer Information Meeting & Training Date for May – week two

School calendars fill up quickly, so January is a good time to request a May date for the Volunteer Meeting & Training. Once you have confirmed availability with the school administration, add this date to the school/grad website and to any upcoming volunteer newsletters/emails so that volunteers "save the date." This meeting is the most important for volunteers as it may be the last before the event, and a lot of information will be covered at that time.

If you have additional training to do, it makes sense to hold that training session on the same night as your volunteer information meeting. This may include training for casino dealers, as well as those who may be running equipment or contests that night. We usually offer our casino training earlier in the evening, followed by an all volunteer information meeting.

AG Committee Meeting – week four

At this meeting, the finance coordinator may be able to present the working budget that was developed using all of the sub-committee Quote Sheets. This is a good time to make adjustments and to review the dollars required to run the AG event.

As well, this consolidated budget will give the fundraising & prizes sub-committee a good sense of what is needed in terms of fundraising dollars.

> *"The best part about having an After-Grad was having all the graduates together in one place for the event. My memories would be foggy and distorted if I didn't have the Safe Grad to enjoy. So many events were happening, that there was always something for everyone to enjoy. The After-Grad left me and my friends with tons of memories and great photos!"*
>
> — Stephanie, graduate

FEBRUARY

February is one of those months where you still feel there is a lot to be done, but you can't really find a lot more to do, at least this I what I find each year when working on the After-Grad. This is a great month to set up the event protocol and create the Grad and Guest Agreements, and to solidify the fundraising efforts and the publicity plan. It's also a great time to reconnect with parents and to make another appeal for volunteers. As things move along, use this time to complete any outstanding action items, because next month is a busy one – once you hit March, time really flies!

FEBRUARY – ACTION ITEMS

Week	Chair	Communications & Publicity Co-ordinator	Finances Co-ordinator	Volunteer Committee	Transportation, Operations & Safety Committee	Decorating, Food & Beverage Committee	Entertainment, Games & Contests Committee	Fundraising & Prizes Committee
WEEK 1	Develop Grad/Guest Agreement & Event Protocol							Solidify Fundraising Solicitations
WEEK 2	Parent Presentation (Solicit Volunteers)							
WEEK 3		Review Publicity & Print Plan						
WEEK 4	AG Committee Meeting	AG Committee Meeting	AG Committee Meeting	AG Committee Meeting	AG Committee Meeting	AG Committee Meeting	AG Committee Meeting	AG Committee Meeting

Sample "Action Items – February" is available as a PDF document or an Excel document at www.safegradevent.com/tools/forms/actionitemsfebruary

 ## CHAIR

Develop Grad/Guest Agreement & Event Protocol – week one

Some AG groups have grads and guests sign agreements or protocol guidelines in advance. Other groups may sell tickets at the event doors, with no prior contact with grads/guests, and may have their guidelines available on their own or a school website and/or posted at the entrance of the event. Whichever method works for your group, the guidelines/protocol for most Dry Grad events are similar.

In order to control the attendance at their event, some AG groups allow only grads and no guests to attend, while others allow guests, but only those attending the same school or a school within their community.

I have included a sample agreement in the book and on the website that you can use for ideas or download and revise as needed. While these are <u>not "legal" documents</u>, they do include some central and important points, and do, when signed by grads/guests and parents, show an understanding, agreement and intent. Having agreements in place does not guarantee that you won't have any problems at the event, but it does provide a set of expectations as well as the grounds for denied entry to or dismissal from the event. Some points to consider as agreement guidelines or event protocol:

- ✓ An understanding/agreement that the After-Grad event may not be/is not a School sponsored event, nor is it authorized or organized by the School, and forms no part of the formal graduating ceremonies, or requirements for attendance or graduation from the School whether or not any School staff attend, assist, or are invited to the AG event.
- ✓ An understanding/agreement and/or permission by the parent for their grad/guest's attendance at the event.
- ✓ Contact information for the parents/guardians during the time of the event.
- ✓ The cost of the ticket and what is included in that cost.

- ✓ All attendants must be identified by an After-Grad wristband.
- ✓ An understanding/agreement of the transportation being provided and any arrangements made for returning the grad/guest to his/her home.
- ✓ The fact that the event is drug and alcohol free (for all attending including those who may be of legal drinking age) and that the behaviour needs to be conducive to a safe, drug-free and alcohol-free celebration.
- ✓ An understanding/agreement that every grad/guest will be searched upon entry and that no non-essential personal articles will be permitted, including any liquids of any kind (unless they represent medication). Any non-permitted items in the grad/guest's possession during the search at the time of event check-in will be submitted to the security personnel for safekeeping until the conclusion of the event. All items will be kept in a secure location, supervised by parent volunteers at all times, and returned prior to leaving the event (excepting illegal items such as drugs/alcohol). Purses/bags/backpacks will be held at the Coat Check and may be accessed but not carried on their person during the event.
- ✓ No alcohol or drugs to be consumed/used or any materials or items (drugs or alcohol) that may affect the grad/guest's behaviour or that may be used to harm others, such as any items that could be considered to be or used as weapons, at any time during the event, including the transfer to/from the event.
- ✓ The expectation that the grad/guest will remain at the event for its entirety and that there are no in/out privileges.
- ✓ An understanding that the School, the Parent Sponsors, along with the onsite Parent Volunteers are not responsible for the grad/guest's actions; grads and guests are responsible for their own actions, including leaving the event site prior to the conclusion of the AG event, with or without the organizers' knowledge or permission.
- ✓ An understanding and agreement that the possession of or showing the effects of drugs, alcohol or weapons will not be tolerated and will constitute grounds for

dismissal from the event. Behaviour that is deemed to be disruptive to the event, will result in detention onsite by Security personnel along with a parent volunteer, until the legal parents/guardians are notified and able to pick up the grad/guest immediately. Parents/guardians are required to sign the student out of the event.

- ✓ Any additional transportation expenses incurred as a result of dismissal from the event will be the sole responsibility of the student/parent/guardian. Any prohibited substance or item found in the student's possession will be confiscated and a report may be filed with the local law enforcement agency, if applicable.
- ✓ Permission for photography/videography that may include the grad/guest and the posting of any/all photographs/videos on the supplier/school/society website.
- ✓ An understanding/agreement that written refund requests may be considered and/or approved at the discretion of the Sponsors only.
- ✓ The provision of any information that might be helpful pertaining to medical conditions/requirements, and food/drug allergies and an agreement that this information may be shared with onsite medical/wellness personnel if required (Doctors, Nurses, Police) and an understanding that emergency medical decisions may be required.
- ✓ An agreement to release and hold harmless the Parent Sponsors/Volunteers, School, the Venue and all agents, employees, and assignees of each for any damages suffered by the parent/guardian or their son/daughter arising from his/her attendance at this event.
- ✓ Home and cell phone contact numbers along with the names of those to whom the grad/guest can be released, with a requirement for appropriate ID upon pickup.

If you are gathering signed agreements in advance, the forms provide an opportunity to secure T-shirt sizes if you are offering commemorative T-shirts/signing at the event – a very popular activity at most After-Grads.

A sample "Grad Agreement" is available in Appendix – Forms and as a PDF document or as a Word document at www.safegradevent.com/tools/forms/gradagreement

A sample "Guest Agreement" is available in Appendix – Forms and as a PDF document or as a Word document at www.safegradevent.com/tools/forms/guestagreement

Parent Presentation (Solicit Volunteers) – week two

If the school administration is having a grad parent meeting this month, ask once again for a spot on the agenda to review the event's progress and to put out another appeal for volunteers. Show your Event Flow that was created in November, and once again, hand out volunteer forms to anyone who has not completed one and secure any missing email addresses. Take questions and mention the May date for Volunteer Information & Training.

COMMUNICATIONS & PUBLICITY

Review Publicity & Print Plan – week three

Now that your local business community is aware of the event, and hopefully supporting your efforts by spreading the positive message, review the publicity plan to make sure everything is on track.

With the money set aside in your budget for printing, you may want to get started on designing the print pieces. Depending on whether or not you are working with the school, you may need to design the casino money and event tickets, so working with the fundraising & prizes sub-committee you can develop a design that works. Signage can also be started now to be ready to place the final order for all print pieces in May.

FUNDRAISING & PRIZES

Solidify Fundraising Solicitations – week one

By now, your message of awareness and need has begun to spread, and you may have heard back from a number of partners who are willing to support the fundraising efforts. Use this time to follow up with local business and community organizations and to arrange the pickup/transfer arrangements, add contact information to your Supplier Contact List, and add to your Thank-You List. Update the finance coordinator, so the budget can be revised and sub-committees can determine if there is extra money available for event add-ons, a tentative ticket price can be set, and everyone can get a sense of what the next few months might bring in terms of income.

> *"Throughout the night I kept on saying how amazing the whole event was. You thought of everything to keep the grads interested and having fun!"*
>
> — Laurie, parent volunteer

MARCH

The home stretch is defined as the final portion of an undertaking and for me that's what March represents – the beginning of that home stretch. Although there are still a few months left, I look forward to this point in the process because it's time to start nailing down the details and put all of the operational pieces into place – the pieces that will actually make the event happen.

At this time of year, I review what has been worked on these past few months. Doing this review now helps you figure out what you may have missed, and with fresh eyes, provides an opportunity to add in anything you feel might add value that you can still afford within your budget. This is a great job for the chair as he/she has been overseeing the various sub-committees since October.

This month, the primary action item for everyone is the creation of an Event Schedule. For any event of this size, it is a must have – one event plan/schedule that includes all the players and captures every event detail. This comprehensive document outlines everyone's responsibilities, what is being provided and by whom and it serves as a great working reference on the night of the event when so much is happening, all at the same time!

MARCH – ACTION ITEMS

Week	Chair	Communications & Publicity Co-ordinator	Finances Co-ordinator	Volunteer Committee	Transportation, Operations & Safety Committee	Decorating, Food & Beverage Committee	Entertainment, Games & Contests Committee	Fundraising & Prizes Committee
Week 1	Progress Review	Confirm Donations from February Follow Up	Budget Review	Create Volunteer Duty Grid	Supplier Touch Base	Supplier Touch Base	Supplier Touch Base	Supplier Touch Base
	Create Event Schedule			Create Event Schedule Section	Create Event Schedule Section	Create Event Schedule Section	Create Event Schedule Section	Create Event Schedule
Week 2				Prepare Volunteer Appeal				
Week 3								
Week 4	AG Committee Meeting	AG Committee Meeting	AG Committee Meeting	AG Committee Meeting	AG Committee Meeting	AG Committee Meeting	AG Committee Meeting	AG Committee Meeting

Sample "Action Items – March" is available as a PDF document or Excel document at www.safegradevent.com/tools/forms/actionitemsmarch

 # CHAIR

Progress Review – week one

As mentioned above, I take time at the beginning of March to review the progress of each sub-committee. There may be outstanding action items that the chair can assist with and this is a good time to determine if everything is on track, and if you are off track there is still plenty of time to make the necessary adjustments.

Create Event Schedule – week one

An Event Schedule is the one document that you will use on the night of the event, that captures every detail of the event. March is a good time to start building the Event Schedule because many of the details become available this month, and by creating it now, you will only be adding in the final touches as you make your way to June.

This form is created as an ongoing Microsoft Word document, and although may seem lengthy, keep in mind that this is the only reference piece you may need on event night. Yours may look quite different than the sample but it gives you an idea of the type of information included and the recommended format.

The easiest way to create the schedule is chronologically and by having each sub-committee complete their own information. The document will grow as everyone fills in their own information. Ask each sub-committee to use a different colour text and when the final document is reviewed in early June, you can turn it all to black and your finished document will be complete and ready to use. As with some of the other documents, you can set this up as a "sharing document" on Google Docs or similar cyber place. And the chair can continue to review the document over the next few months, while the volunteer names can be added in late May or early June.

A sample "Event Schedule" is available in Appendix – Forms and as a PDF document or as a Word document at www.safegradevent.com/tools/forms/eventschedule

COMMUNICATIONS & PUBLICITY

Confirm Donations from February Follow Up – week one

As we are now about 3 or 4 months away from the event, this may be a good time to revisit the businesses, organizations and individuals that you contacted in February to reiterate the need for funding/donations. It may help to work together with the Fundraising & Prizes sub-committee on this action item.

 FINANCE

Budget Review – week one

If you have not been reviewing your budget regularly, now is a good time to revisit this working document. Once you have a current budget number, you can let the other coordinators and sub-committee chairs know at this month's meeting if they have any extra funds available for additional event items. Keep your "ideal" ticket price in mind as extra funds can be used to reduce that fee rather than add features to the event.

 VOLUNTEER

Create Volunteer Duty Grid – week one

Creating a Volunteer Grid in March provides you with plenty of time to determine what spots you still need to fill and whether or not you need to send out a second appeal.

The sample grid lists the positions that we used for our 2010 event, and you may have many of the same, and some different positions. If your volunteers have indicated on their Volunteer Forms, what area they would like to work in and/or how much time they can dedicate to the event, fill in those positions first.

For those volunteers who may not be able to commit to joining you on the night of the event, they may be able to give some time in the early morning to help with the tearing down and clean up of the event. Because we tear down some rooms in the early hours, and clean up as we go, we have few morning clean-up requirements, but that may not be the case for all event groups, especially for larger groups, or those where the venue does not supply janitorial services.

Begin recording names based on the information you have collected on your Volunteer Forms as well as any additional information from meetings. Keep in mind that there are various time slots, and some overlap which will allow some volunteers to assist with multiple duties during the event. For example, someone who helps set up decorating early on, could then serve "mocktails" at the beginning of the event, and then take a shift in the nightclub later on, before escorting a bus home. Other volunteers, like casino dealers, often stay in one position for the entire event.

Your list of activities and events will determine your volunteer positions and the job description for each along with the time commitment for that position. In addition to those listed in our template, if you are offering "outside" activities, you may require additional volunteers to supervise activities or to patrol the outside perimeter.

We work hard each year to make sure that our parent/student ratio is less than

20% – you don't want it to look like there are more adults than students at a student After-Grad!

A sample "Volunteer Grid" is available in Appendix – Forms and as a PDF document or as an Excel document at www.safegradevent.com/tools/forms/volunteergrid

Create Event Schedule Section – week one

At this point, you may want to slot the names of the volunteers from your grid into the Event Schedule, or you may choose to wait until later in May, or early June. If you have a pretty solid grid and many of the positions are filled, it makes sense to get it done now. But if you are going to send out another appeal for more volunteers, it may be worth waiting to see how it all unfolds, so you are not doing double the work later on, to move names around.

You can either work with the shared document that the chair has created, or you can use the sample "Event Schedule" available in Appendix – Forms and as a PDF document or as a Word document at www.safegradevent.com/tools/forms/eventschedule

Remember to use colours other than black, so that later on when you combine the information from all sub-committees on this form, it's easy to see each member's contribution.

Prepare Volunteer Appeal – week two

If you find, once you have populated the grid with volunteer names that you need more volunteers, you can launch a second email appeal. You may know what specific positions need to be filled, so be specific if you can, and once you have secured more names, you can go back to your grid and may even be able to complete it.

TRANSPORTATION, OPERATIONS, & SAFETY

Supplier Touch Base – week one

It may have been several months since you first spoke to your suppliers and now is a good time to follow up and firm up any tentative bookings, selecting those you can afford and want to include, and releasing those that you can't afford or have decided are not the right fit for whatever reason. When touching base and confirming supplier involvement, reconfirm the pricing you agreed upon when the quote was first provided and ask again about any onsite requirements.

At this time, you may be asked to sign contracts and/or pay deposits, and by now, the budget should be firm enough so that you can make those decisions and payments.

Make sure you know the applicable cancellation/penalty fees that may be incurred if the event cancels for any reason, however unlikely it may be.

Remember to update your Quote Sheet and any Contact Lists with any new/changed information.

Create Event Schedule Section– week one

At this point, you may want to slot in the timing and needs that pertain to those volunteers that will be assisting with your area. You don't need to know the volunteer names but you do need to complete any information regarding the venue, event operation, transportation, and safety and security. You can fill in any outstanding information as it becomes available.

You can either work with the shared document that the chair has created, or you can use the sample "Event Schedule" available in Appendix – Forms and as a PDF document or as a Word document at www.safegradevent.com/tools/forms/eventschedule

Remember to use a colour other than black, so that later on when you combine the information from all sub-committees on this form, it's easy to see each member's contribution.

DECORATING, FOOD & BEVERAGE

Supplier Touch Base – week one

It may have been several months since you first spoke to your suppliers and now is a good time to follow up and firm up any tentative bookings, selecting those you can afford and want to include, and releasing those that you can't afford or have decided are not the right fit for whatever reason. When touching base and confirming supplier involvement, reconfirm the pricing you agreed upon when the quote was first provided and ask again, about any onsite requirements.

At this time, you may be asked to sign contracts and/or pay deposits, and by now, the budget should be firm enough so that you can make those decisions and payments. Make sure you know the applicable cancellation/penalty fees that may be incurred if the event cancels for any reason, however unlikely that may be.

Remember to update your Quote Sheet and any Contact Lists with any new/changed information.

Create Event Schedule Section – week one

At this point, you may want to slot in the timing and needs that pertain to those volunteers who will be assisting with your area. You don't need to know the volunteer names but you do need to complete any information regarding the decorating and food & beverage. You can fill in any outstanding information as it becomes available.

You can either work with the shared document that the chair has created, or you can use the sample "Event Schedule" available in Appendix – Forms and as a PDF document or as a Word document at www.safegradevent.com/tools/forms/eventschedule

Remember to use a colour other than black, so that later on when you combine the information from all sub-committees on this form, it's easy to see each member's contribution

ENTERTAINMENT, GAMES & CONTESTS

Supplier Touch Base – week one

It may have been several months since you first spoke to your suppliers and now is a good time to follow up and firm up any tentative bookings, selecting those you can afford and want to include, and releasing those that you can't afford or have decided are not the right fit for whatever reason. When touching base and confirming supplier involvement, reconfirm the pricing you agreed upon when the quote was first provided and ask again about any particular onsite requirements.

At this time, you may be asked to sign contracts and/or pay deposits. By now the budget should be firm enough so that you can make those decisions and payments. Make sure you know the applicable cancellation/penalty fees that may be incurred if the event cancels for any reason, however unlikely that may be.

Remember to update your Quote Sheet and any Contact Lists with any new/changed information.

Create Event Schedule Section– week one

At this point, you may want to slot in the timing and needs that pertain to those volunteers who will be assisting with your area. You don't need to know the volunteer names but you do need to complete any information regarding the venue, event operation, transportation, and safety and security. You can fill in any outstanding information as it becomes available.

You can either work with the shared document that the chair has created, or you can use the "Event Schedule" available in Appendix – Forms and as a PDF document or as a Word document at www.safegradevent.com/tools/forms/eventschedule

Remember to use a colour other than black, so that later on when you combine the information from all sub-committees on this form, it's easy to see each member's contribution.

 FUNDRAISING & PRIZES

Supplier Touch Base – week one

It may have been several months since you first spoke to your suppliers and now is a good time to follow up and firm up any tentative bookings, selecting those you can afford and want to include, and releasing those that you can't afford or have decided are not the right fit for whatever reason. When touching base and confirming supplier involvement, reconfirm the pricing you agreed upon when the quote was first provided and ask again about any onsite requirements.

At this time, you may be asked to sign contracts and/or pay deposits. By now the budget should be firm enough so that you can make those decisions and payments. Make sure you know the applicable cancellation/penalty fees that may be incurred if the event cancels for any reason, however unlikely that may be.

Remember to update your Quote Sheet and any Contact Lists which any new/changed information.

Create Event Schedule Section – week one

At this point, you may want to slot in the timing and needs that pertain to those volunteers who will be assisting with your area. You don't need to know the volunteer names but you do need to complete any information regarding the prize draw and any other onsite event advertising/signage or donor recognition. You can fill in any outstanding information as it becomes available.

You can either work with the shared document that the chair has created, or you can use the sample "Event Schedule" available in Appendix – Forms and as a PDF document or as a Word document at www.safegradevent.com/tools/forms/eventschedule

Remember to use a colour other than black, so that later on when you combine the information from all sub-committees on this form, it's easy to see each member's contribution.

> *"[The After-Grad] brings everyone closer together and helps the barriers of groups come down finally. It is something that non-drinkers or partiers can look forward to. I think that the time you get to spend with everyone is so amazing and I wouldn't trade that for anything. The most important thing is that no one in my graduation class died that night."*
>
> — Caleigh, graduate

APRIL

In early April, our school administration presents an "information meeting" to the grad class and distributes a "graduation package" with all of the paperwork associated with Graduation Day. I use this opportunity to present the final After-Grad plan to the students, to build excitement and keep the momentum going, and as a promotional opportunity to those who have not yet decided to attend. It's a chance to remind them that this event has something for everyone, and truly will be a night they don't want to miss, where every grad feels "included" and lifelong memories are made.

Include in the school package, general After-Grad information and the Grad and Guest Agreements/Protocol that you prepared last month.

If you are preparing a separate package from the school, request an opportunity during a grad class presentation to provide your package – it is so much easier if the class is already gathered together.

APRIL – ACTION ITEMS

Week	Chair	Communications & Publicity Co-ordinator	Finances Co-ordinator	Volunteer Committee	Transportation, Operations & Safety Committee	Decorating, Food & Beverage Committee	Entertainment, Games & Contests Committee	Fundraising & Prizes Committee
Week 1		Distribute AG Agreements						
Week 2	Assist Communications Coordinator with Promotion			Update Volunteer Grid				
Week 3		Review Signage & Print Pieces, Place Orders			Reconfirm Wellness & Security Teams	Source "leftover" F&B options		
		Review AG Agreements & Create AG Binder						
Week 4					Create Installation Schedule	Create Floor Plans	Create Floor Plans	
	AG Committee Meeting	AG Committee Meeting	AG Committee Meeting	AG Committee Meeting	AG Committee Meeting	AG Committee Meeting	AG Committee Meeting	AG Committee Meeting

Sample "Action Items – April" is available as a PDF document or an Excel document at www.safegradevent.com/tools/forms/actionitemsapril

 CHAIR

Assist Communications Coordinator with Promotion – week two

This month, there is time to help with promotion of the event. Work with the communications sub-committee to contact local media, update the event/school website and continue to spread the word.

COMMUNICATIONS & PUBLICITY

Distribute AG Agreements/Forms – week one

As mentioned in the intro to this month, we include our Grad and Guest Agreements in the school package that goes out to all Grade 12 students. If that opportunity is not available to you, you can set up a time at the school to distribute them, have the grad exec group assist you, or have parents pick them up at a designated time/place.

Using a school grade 12 grad student list will help identify how many packages you need, and labelling them will identify the leftovers after the initial distribution.

As with the surveys, ask the school or PAC for a mailbox that you can share or use. And allow between 2 to 3 weeks for forms to be returned. If you give too much time, the packages find their way into corners of the bedroom, never to be seen again. And, the sooner the return date, the more time you have to review them and gather any outstanding information as well as follow up on strays.

Review Signage & Print Pieces, Place Orders – week three

Work with the Communications & Publicity sub-committee (who began work on the print design in February), to place orders for signage and other print pieces. If you are concerned about last-minute changes, you can wait until early May to place the orders, but check on your supplier's timelines to be sure your pieces will be ready for your event date.

Review AG Agreements & Create AG Binder - week four

As the completed agreements arrive, review them to make sure you have everything you need, complete information, signatures, etc. File the agreements alphabetically by grad's last name and either include the guest form alongside, or set up a separate section within the binder for guests only.

VOLUNTEER

Update Volunteer Grid - week two

Following your second appeal, you can now complete the grid. In May you will have an opportunity to advise all the volunteers of their assigned positions and make changes to the grid as needed. This may be a good time to ask for those volunteers who might be willing to wear a costume, as the level of willingness may affect who does what/when. Try to put costumes on volunteers who will have interaction with the grads/guests, such as food vendors, casino dealers, etc.

TRANSPORTATION, OPERATIONS & SAFETY

Reconfirm Wellness and Security Teams - week three

It has been many weeks since you last made contact with these teams so this is a good time to email or call each team member to touch base and reconfirm their involvement. They may have questions and you will have more information available to answer those questions a month out from the event.

Create Installation Schedule – week four

Many suppliers for the event will want to install their equipment or deliver their rentals during the daytime business hours on event day. And, the venue may have "delivery times" and may or may not require a committee member to be onsite during delivery. If your committee members have grads, they will be busy enough on grad day, and may not be available to handle the deliveries. If you have a good schedule, you can enlist the help of a non-grad parent while you are with your own graduate that day.

Floor plans will have also been drawn up this week, so enlist the help of both the decorating and entertainment sub-committees to provide the "location" for suppliers. Much of the information you need for the schedule is available on the Supplier Contact list you started back in November.

A sample "Installation Schedule" is available in Appendix – Forms and as a PDF document or as an Excel document at www.safegradevent.com/tools/forms/installationschedule

DECORATING, FOOD & BEVERAGE

Source "Leftover" F&B Options – week three

Depending on your Food & Beverage provider, there may be an opportunity to use rather than waste non-perishable food & beverage leftovers from the event. You will need to check with the venue and your F&B provider about the "rules" concerning food distribution. Your local food bank and community organizations may also be helpful in determining if there is a need in your community and a system to handle the distribution. The school may also be able to use these donations, especially if there is a cafeteria or foods program in your school.

Create Floor Plans - week four

Floor plans are important and you will be glad you have them on the day of your event. They don't need to be sophisticated, and can even be hand-drawn. Many venues will have floor plans for their event spaces, and if not, they should at least be able to provide the necessary room dimensions along with a list of existing stationary items (items that are permanent and can't be moved), and power sources. You can simply draw in your items right on to those floor plans.

Not only will floor plans help you, they may be helpful and are often required by suppliers. Those that are installing structures such as a karaoke stage, arcade game, casino tables, buffet tables, and food vendors will need to know how much space is available to them. And you will want to know how much space or how big a footprint those suppliers are going to need/make too, so that you have room for your guests to move around the rooms for maximum comfort and enjoyment. You don't want your tattoo line-up merging with your pizza line-up – that could get messy!

When preparing floor plans, you will need to consult with those on the entertainment sub-committee as they are the other group that will be contributing to floor plans and your/their decisions will impact each other. Each year we assign one room as a lounge/games room, one as a casino, one as a nightclub (we are lucky to have a permanent nightclub space available at our venue), and the main concourse as a "street" or open entertainment space.

Whether or not you will have as many separate spaces for your event, you need to give some thought to the placement of your themed decorating pieces as well as buffet tables. If you have the supplier's space requirements or footprint information, you will know how much space is required. We include a buffet in every space, but you may want to only include them in a couple of rooms, especially if space is limited. Give consideration to the event flow/timing and traffic flow to determine the best sites for Food & Beverage.

As you work your way through the floor plans making placement decisions, keep these in mind:

- ✓ Existing pieces (for example, a piano) can oftentimes be moved although there may be a charge.
- ✓ Consider your seating needs – we try to not have too much as we want the grads/guests to stay engaged in the event, move from room to room, and keep the flow going. We do generally offer seating for 1/3 of the group.
- ✓ Consider the need for dining tables – we offer only finger foods, limited seating and some side tables but no dining tables – they are an added expense and also take up valuable room that can be used for an activity or entertainment.
- ✓ Consider your power needs, where do you need to plug something in, such as an air hockey game or speakers for karaoke.
- ✓ Consider the logistics of loading in and placement of items – moving an arcade game up a few stairs can be difficult, and pillars can get in the way of a large billiards table.
- ✓ Consider the locations of fire exits, washrooms, kitchens, as these can affect placement.
- ✓ Consider items that are existing or permanent and how they can add to the space, such as large plants, showcases, signs, desks and counters.

A sample "Floorplan" (one of our 2010 floor plans) is available in Appendix – Forms and as a PDF document or as a Word document at www.safegradevent.com/forms/floorplan. While it is particular to our venue and event, it will give you an idea of how floorplans might look.

ENTERTAINMENT, GAMES & CONTESTS

Create Floor Plans – week four

Floor plans are essential to have on the day of your event. They don't need to be sophisticated, and can even be hand-drawn. Many venues will have floor plans for their event spaces, and if not, they should at least be able to provide the necessary room dimensions along with a list of existing stationary items (items that are permanent and can't be moved). You can simply draw in your items right on those floor plans.

Not only will floor plans help you, they will be necessary for most suppliers. Those that are installing structures such as a karaoke stage, arcade game and casino tables will need to know how much space is available to them. And you will want to know how much space or how big a footprint those suppliers are going to need/make too, so that you have room for the grads to move around the rooms for maximum comfort, safety and enjoyment.

You will need to consult with members of the decorating, food & beverage sub-committee as they are the other group that will be contributing to floor plans and your/their decisions will impact each other.

If you do not have many separate spaces for your event, you need to give some thought to sound transfer (for example, you can't have the karaoke beside a noisy arcade game). Once you have the space requirements or footprint information, you will know how much space to assign each game/activity.

Each year we assign one room as a lounge/games room, one as a casino, one as a nightclub (we are lucky to have a permanent nightclub space available at our venue), and the main concourse as a "street" or open entertainment space.

Try to create a focus for each space and then imagine what is going on in each space, and what will make the experience in that room even better. For those activities that I think will be popular and have longer line-ups, I always have something nearby for those who are waiting. I put a *TWISTER* game near the photo booth, a video game beside the tattoo booth, etc.

As you work your way through the floor plans making placement decisions, there are a number of things to keep in mind (see complete list in Food & Beverage – week four, page 105).

A sample Floorplan (one of our 2010 floor plans) is available in Appendix – Forms and as a PDF document or as a Word document at www.safegradevent.com/forms/floorplan. While it is particular to our venue and event, it will give you an idea of how floorplans might look.

> *"It was so much fun; it gave the entire class a great opportunity to have fun without worrying about drunken people ruining it. I will never forget it, and wouldn't have missed it for the world."*
>
> — Lindsay, graduate

MAY

May signals that graduation is just around the corner! This is the month where I first start to lose sleep (just kidding). I use this month to fine-tune the event and to complete any forms that were started earlier. By now, you have most of the information you need and your budget is firmly in place, so very little will change from now on.

Depending on your event date, you may have as little as five or as much as eight weeks left before your After-Grad. Either way, with so much already accomplished you should be starting to feel very good about the event and able to envision what it's all going to look like in June. This month is a busy one!

MAY – ACTION ITEMS

Week	Chair	Communications & Publicity Co-ordinator	Finances Co-ordinator	Volunteer Committee	Transportation, Operations & Safety Committee	Decorating, Food & Beverage Committee	Entertainment, Games & Contests Committee	Fundraising & Prizes Committee
WEEK 1						Complete F&B Order		
					Create & Distribute Supplier Agreements	Create & Distribute Supplier Agreements	Create & Distribute Performer Agreements	Create & Distribute Supplier Agreements
WEEK 2		Print & Sell/Distribute Event Tickets			Order Wristbands & Radios		Order Novelty Items & Contest Props	Develop Prize Budget & Allocation List
WEEK 3		Create Master Attendance List		Distribute Volunteer Grid			Order T-shirts & Update Master Guest List	
		Create Master Guest List						
WEEK 4		Send Out/Receive Insurance Certificates		Facilitate Volunteer Meeting & Training Session				
				Place Costume Order	Follow Up on Supplier Invoices, Order Payments	Follow Up on Supplier Invoices, Order Payments	Follow Up on Supplier Invoices, Order Payments	Follow Up on Supplier Invoices, Order Payments
	AG Committee Meeting & Thank Yous	AG Committee Meeting & Thank-Yous	AG Committee Meeting & Thank-Yous	AG Committee Meeting & Thank-Yous	AG Committee Meeting & Thank-Yous	AG Committee Meeting & Thank-Yous	AG Committee Meeting & Thank-Yous	AG Committee Meeting & Thank-Yous

Sample "Action Items – May" is available as a PDF document or an Excel document at www.safegradevent.com/tools/forms/actionitemsmay

COMMUNICATIONS & PUBLICITY

Print & Sell/Distribute Event Tickets – week two

Now is the time to make arrangements for ticket printing. They don't need to be elaborate or expensive. We have been fortunate to have ours printed each year along with the school-sponsored dinner/dance tickets, so we have not had to incur additional printing costs. There are lots of quick print options out there (computer generated tickets), and a local business may offer to do them at a significantly reduced price or as a sponsor, so be sure to check with local print shops.

Once tickets are printed, arrange to have them sold/distributed at the school, by setting aside a lunch hour or after school time slot, when students can purchase their tickets from a committee member. Match your 'sold' list to your grad and guest agreements, so you can track down those who indicated they wanted to attend, but have not purchased or picked up a ticket. Keep a sheet in the AG binder to record tickets that have been collected. Be sure to include the date and timing of the event, the cost, and any other important information on the ticket. If instead, you are selling tickets at the door, then you can arrange printing and hold on to the tickets until the night of the event. These tickets will then be exchanged for wristbands on the night of the event.

You may also want to have name tags on hand for your volunteer group and/or grads/guests, but these need not be commercially printed, because labels can be purchased and the name tags written up at the event, or pre-printed on a computer/printer.

Create the Master Attendance List – week three

Not all venues request an attendance list; however I always create one each year. It is important for the venue to know how many people are in attendance at any one time for fire regulations, and in case of an emergency or evacuation situation. This list should include everyone onsite, including all students, volunteers, and performers and suppliers. We create two lists, one that is alpha by last name, and one that categorizes the type of individual, again in alpha order. This list is also one that is shared within the sub-committees so can be set up online so that others can access it and update it.

If you are selling tickets at the door of the event, you may not know who is attending prior to the event. Ask the school for an accurate list of grads so you have a master list to work with, and as grads gain entrance to the event, you can record their inclusion on the master list, and provide this to the venue, once registration is complete and the entrance closes down. You may want to require identification in the form of a driver's license or student ID to be sure you are admitting the grad who is listed.

A sample "Master Attendance List" is available in Appendix – Forms and as a PDF document or as an Excel document at www.safegradevent.com/tools/forms/masterattendance

Create the Master Guest List – week three

For the sake of simplicity and so that all volunteers are working with the same document, I use one "check off" list for the entire event. It's created now so that T-shirts can be ordered, and then used again at the event.

The list we use includes every possible grad name (by the time June comes, some will not be graduating and still others may choose not to attend the After-Grad), a box for an accompanying guest's name, T-shirt sizes for both grad and guest, T-shirt pickup checkbox for both, medical alerts and exit alerts for both, and notes. We sort the list alphabetically by grad, and we put the guest name alongside that grad, rather than on its own in alpha order as the grad and guest are usually together when arriving or leaving the event, and it makes it easier for reference purposes at the event.

We use the "medical" and "exit" alert columns to indicate grads/guests who have shown food or medical issues/concerns or have exit instructions that differ than the group transfer. We mark those columns with an "x" only, and the information itself stays in the AG Binder and remains confidential.

A sample "Master Guest List" is available in Appendix – Forms and as a PDF document or as an Excel document at www.safegradevent.com/tools/forms/masterguest

Send Out/Receive Insurance Certificates – week four

With Supplier Agreements now in the hands of all suppliers (see all sub-committees – week one), it is likely that they have been forwarding copies of their insurance certificates. Use this time to follow up on any that are outstanding, and forward a copy of your event insurance policy by fax or email to your venue. The venue may also want to see those Supplier Insurance Certificates which you can send at this time.

 VOLUNTEER

Distribute Volunteer Grid – week three

You have been working on the Volunteer Grid for some time, so by now, all of your positions should have a name attached, and you are ready to distribute the grid. Sending it out gives everyone a final opportunity to review their commitment, and for you to make any necessary adjustments.

Facilitate Volunteer Meeting and Training Session – week four

In May, we combine a volunteer meeting with a volunteer training session where we offer training to our volunteer casino dealers (you set this date back in January). For all other volunteer positions, training onsite the night of the event has been sufficient. Many parents may already be familiar with the rules of the various casino games, but training provides a great refresher and allows parents to meet the other volunteers who will be working alongside them as casino dealers.

At this meeting, you can also determine costume sizes for those brave volunteers who have offered to dress in "theme". Our casino dealers have been outfitted with black vests and visors for more formal/elegant themes, or loud flowered shirts & leis for our tropical theme, along with costumed mermaids and pirates in 2010.

The volunteer meeting portion of the evening includes every volunteer associated with the event. This is a final opportunity to confirm everyone's position, fill vacancies, and answer any questions, as well as record cell phone numbers for all lead/supervisory positions. The next time you meet this group will be on the evening of the event, just prior to the grads' arrival, so try to use this meeting to cover off as much as possible.

I present the Event Flow again, along with the finalized floor plans, as many will not be familiar with the venue. It helps everyone visualize the sheer size of the event and the amount of space used. You can also give out driving directions and parking instructions along with maps if needed or you can send these out next month in the Information Email. I have always found this meeting to be informative and a great bonding session for this group of dedicated and supportive parents.

Place Costume Order – week four

If you have included themed costumes in your event, and have your sizing information, you can now place your order. Have your costumes picked up or delivered directly to the venue, so that they are ready for the volunteers when they arrive. Local costume shops as well as theatre groups and dance/drama schools are a great resource for costumes. Remember that these costumes will also need to be returned/picked up following the event.

TRANSPORTATION, OPERATIONS & SAFETY

Create and Distribute Supplier Agreements – week one

As Martha Stewart would say, Supplier Agreements are a "good thing." I use them because they spell out everything that a supplier needs to know about the event, provide all of the event details along with an opportunity to ask questions, point out misunderstandings or misinformation, and it gives you an opportunity to solidify your expectations. Don't forget that, in some cases, you may have not spoken to a transportation supplier in months, so this concise but detailed document becomes their blueprint

As an event planner, there is nothing worse than a transportation supplier with an arrival time that is 30 minutes out from what you thought you had discussed – so the more communication the better. By sending these agreements out in early May, you have time to answer questions and to react to any challenges that a supplier throws your way. And, when working on your agreement, you will find out very quickly what you have forgotten or don't know, such as installation timing for a venue, or parking restrictions, etc.

Included in the Supplier Agreement are the terms for payment. Ask for an invoice complete with all contact information and pricing including all taxes. I give suppliers two weeks and then in week four I follow up – some payments won't be made until following the event, but many can be made on the night of the event or immediately following. Having the invoice early gives you time to verify its accuracy.

A sample "Supplier Agreement" is available in Appendix – Forms and as a PDF document or as a Word document at www.safegradevent.com/tools/forms/supplieragreement

Order Wristbands & Radios – week two

All AG events should use a wristband system, and as mentioned earlier, it's a requirement for most insurers. Before placing your order, check with the entertainment sub-committee as they are also making purchases this week for their novelty items and may be working with a company that also provides wristbands. Failing that, you can place your own order, and my recommendation is to use coloured bands. There are even themed bands available, but we keep it simple, and use plain coloured bands. If you are moving the whole group on the return transfer in the morning (as opposed to having guests picked up) on buses, you may want to colour code your groups when they first enter the event.

You will know the bus capacities from your transportation quote/contract, so leaving two seats available for escorts, assign the balance of bus seats to one colour for each bus. For example, we used five buses in 2010 so we had five groups of 45 (we had 47-passenger buses). When guests arrive to the event, the first 45 received one colour, then the next 45 got a new colour and so on (make sure grads enter with their guests so they ride home together). In the morning, you simply direct the purple wristband guests to the bus with the purple sign, and orange wristbands board the orange bus, etc. If you have signed in the guests the night before, and written the colour beside their name, you have a perfect bus list or manifest in the morning without having to sign anyone out. Plus you will also know if you are missing anyone – if your bus is not full, you can do a roll call and figure out who is still inside the venue.

Follow Up on Supplier Invoices, Order Payments – week three

Hopefully you have received a few invoices by now. If not, you can follow up and remind suppliers that you can't arrange to pay them until you have an invoice in your hands. Your sub-committee will need to check the invoice for accuracy before forwarding it on to the finance coordinator to arrange for payment. Payments will be made at various times: some during daytime installation, some entertainers on event night, and others will be paid immediately following the event. In any case, the more invoices you have in your hands, the faster those payments can be made – you don't want to be paying out invoices in July, long after schools are closed and committee members are on vacation. It's a good thing for each sub-committee to keep track of their own suppliers since you have built that relationship, rather than having the finance coordinator try to track them down, weeks later.

DECORATING, FOOD & BEVERAGE

Complete F&B Order – week one

By now you may have an idea of your group size, either based on Agreements that were received, past event numbers, or an estimate based on your current grad class size.

Based on that number, you can select a preliminary menu that might be a good fit for the event. If you are tied into the venue's own F&B operation you can review their menus, or if you are working with local restaurants or grocers, you can consult with them to create a preliminary list and you may even have the flexibility to change your order right up to the day of the event. Your F&B provider will know how much food is required for a six to seven hour event and for the size of group, so rely on their expertise. This should be a preliminary order at this stage, one that will need to be guaranteed closer to the event. It will give you a good idea of cost at this point and there shouldn't be too many changes to guest numbers.

Remember to consider the timing of your event, and what has happened earlier in the day. In our case, the group is coming directly from their dinner/dance, so they have eaten dinner about five hours prior to arriving at the After-Grad. Our group is not too hungry upon arrival, but enjoys a welcome/signature "mocktail" along with canapés, or finger foods prior to hitting the buffets. If your event is a standalone event, you will need to take into consideration whether or not a heavier menu is appropriate.

If you are working with grad and/or guest Agreements, you will know who has food restrictions/allergies and can make your food provider aware so that options can be made available to those students.

Based on your group size and available budget, create an initial F&B Order. Don't be shy; ask your food provider for help, as he/she will know how many mini-wraps or pizza slices your group might eat. Keep your budget in mind and your F&B percentages and don't over-buy. It's easy to get carried away and order far more food than you need.

Remember to speak to your supplier about how you are handling leftovers, and ask them to keep track of what is left/not eaten at the event, so you can provide that information for next year's committee. You don't want to waste money or food, so rely on your suppliers and any historical information you have when making your selections.

The idea is to have food readily available to the grads all night long, to help keep them hydrated and fuelled, and feeling well and energized. We generally average one drink per guest per hour, so we offer lots of water as well as juice, soft drinks, and then coffee in the early morning hours. Staying hydrated means staying awake, and free of headaches. As mentioned earlier, we don't allow any liquids to be brought into the event, for safety reasons, and we don't offer "energy" drinks – again, trying to maintain overall wellness and reduce the incidence of headaches, etc. We choose foods that appeal to teens, including healthy foods with protein along with vegetarian options to help keep the energy up, meanwhile limiting the sugar to help keep the headaches down. We emphasize snack style and finger foods that are easy to pick up on the way into the next room or next activity, can be eaten while standing in line for an activity, and limited or no cutlery.

The buffets are ready to go as soon as the event begins and we provide one in every room or event space, including the main concourse, with identical food and beverages available on each. This allows grads to stay in a particular area they are enjoying without having to go far to find food – it has to be accessible and easy to find. In the casino, we have the food brought to the players by volunteer servers – often dressed to suit the theme. The grads don't have to leave the poker table, where they might be winning, even if they are hungry. We also continuously pass out bottled water in the casino for the same reason.

Don't forget to include your volunteers and suppliers in your order. Our suppliers don't usually eat in the early morning hours, so we provide beverages as needed. We provide the volunteer food in the Volunteer//Wellness room, including sandwiches, deli trays, and beverages, and volunteers also have access to the buffets. Most adults don't eat a great deal in the early morning so it has not affected our menu order, however, depending on your attendance numbers, it could. Some events have 40 or 50 volunteers like ours, but large events or those that invite multiple schools can have up to 300 or more volunteers, and that can add up on the buffet table or the coffee line.

Some schools opt to add breakfast items to their menu. For the early morning departure, we provide only a few items on the buses instead. In our first year, we provided coffee, fruit juice, whole fruits and muffins, and we had tremendous waste. The students are far too tired to think about breakfast, and some will have just finished a 4:30 am slice of pizza! In recent years, we have provided bottled water, extra juices, and a few granola bars on the ride home which seems to work very well. At this point, sleep is preferable to food – an unusual twist for teens!

As an example of an F&B order, I have included our list for F&B in 2009 (a group of 200 grads and guests). In addition to what was provided by the venue, we supplemented this list with hot dogs and fresh popcorn.

Upon Arrival

- ✓ 4 large crudités & dip (leftovers go to buffets) – serves 120
- ✓ 6 small tortilla chips & salsa (leftovers to buffets) – serves 60
- ✓ 6 punch bowls of "Pink Panther" signature mocktail – serves 210

Main Concourse & Each Buffet

- ✓ 40 large pizzas – 4 flavour options – serves 320 slices
- ✓ 4 large fruit platters – serves 120
- ✓ 4 large deli platters – serves 120

Dessert Items

- ✓ 160 small cookies
- ✓ 100 granola bars

Volunteers & Suppliers

- ✓ 1 large deli platter – serves 30
- ✓ 1 large sandwich tray (15) – serves 15 to 30

Beverages

- ✓ 400 bottled water
- ✓ 320 soft drinks
- ✓ 100 bottled fruit juice
- ✓ 10 pots of coffee – serves 100

Our sample "F&B Order" is available in Appendix – Forms and as a PDF document or as an Excel document at www.safegradevent.com/tools/forms/fandborder

Create and Distribute Supplier Agreements – week one

As Martha Stewart would say, Supplier Agreements are a "good thing." I use them because they spell out everything that a supplier needs to know about the event, provide all of the event details, and provide the supplier with an opportunity to ask questions, point out misunderstandings or misinformation, and it gives you an opportunity to solidify your expectations. Don't forget that in some cases, you may have not spoken to a rental company in months, so this concise but detailed document becomes their blueprint.

As an event planner, it is frustrating and embarrassing to have a rental company delivering blue linens, when in your last discussion four months ago, you were sure you had agreed on black – so the more precise communication the better. By sending these Agreements out in early May, you have time to answer questions and to adjust to any challenges that a supplier throws your way. And, when working on your Agreement, you will find out very quickly, what you have forgotten or don't know, such as installation timing for table linens, or an additional charge for mocktail glasses.

Included in the Agreement are the terms for payment. Ask for an invoice complete with all contact information and pricing including all taxes. I give suppliers two weeks and then follow-up in week 4 – some payments won't be made until following the event, but many can be made on the night of the event so having the invoice early gives you time to verify its accuracy and request a cheque.

A sample "Supplier Agreement" is available in Appendix – Forms and as a PDF document or as a Word document at www.SafeGradEvent.com/forms/supplieragreement

Follow Up on Supplier Invoices, Order Payments – week three

Hopefully you have received a few invoices by now. If not, you can follow up and remind suppliers that you can't pay them until you have an invoice in your hands. Your sub-committee will need to check the invoice for accuracy before forwarding it on to your finance coordinator to arrange for payment. Payments will be made at various times: some during daytime installation, some entertainers on event night, and others will be paid immediately following the event. In any case, the more invoices you have in your hands, the more promptly those payments can be made – you don't want to be paying out invoices in July, long after schools are closed and committee members are on vacation. It's a good thing for each sub-committee to keep track of their own suppliers since you have built that relationship, rather than having the finance coordinator have to track them down, weeks later.

ENTERTAINMENT, GAMES, & CONTESTS

Create & Distribute Performer Agreements – week one

Performer Agreements are definitely a "good thing." We use them because they spell out everything that an entertainer needs to know about the event, provide all of the event details, and provide the entertainer with an opportunity to ask questions, point out misunderstandings or misinformation, and it gives you an opportunity to solidify your expectations. Don't forget that in some cases, you may have not spoken to this person in months, so this concise but detailed document becomes their blueprint.

As an event planner, there are few things worse than a band showing up in their jeans for a formal affair, or a juggler bringing the fire sticks the venue clearly banned – the more detailed communication the better. By sending these Agreements out in early May, you have time to answer questions and to adjust to any challenges that a supplier throws your way. And, when working on your Agreement, you will find out very quickly, what you have forgotten or don't know, such as 'play time' for a band, or additional expenses for the DJ's smoke machine.

Included in the Agreement are the terms for payment. Ask for an invoice complete with all contact information pricing including all taxes. We give suppliers two weeks and then follow-up in week four – some payments won't be made until following the event, but many can be made on the night of the event and having the invoice early gives you time to verify its accuracy.

A sample "Performer Agreement" is available in Appendix – Forms and as a PDF document or as a Word document at www.safegradevent.com/tools/forms/performeragreeement

Order Novelty Items & Contest Props – week two

I always wait until May to order novelty items and contest props, for a few reasons. Since contest props can be used and then returned, loaned items may work well or you can purchase them and then give them away following the event. For our 2010 AG event, we purchased a limbo pole, some hula hoops and some costumes for a beach relay – all of these items then made their way to a children's pre-school following the event. And by now you may have a better idea of guest numbers, and you hopefully have some funds available to pay these invoices..

Traditionally I have ordered my novelty items and contest props online, buying a mix of three or four novelty items for each gender, with each guest receiving one novelty.

Online shopping may require a credit card; your school may be willing to make the purchase on your behalf, or your society may have its own credit card available for use. I have always enjoyed very quick delivery on all of my items, so by ordering now, you are sure to be able to have everything in hand in time for the event and enough time for last minute orders as well

Make sure you have checked with all sub-committees in case they have an item you can include in your order, as a larger order may provide a volume discount and save on shipping costs.

Order T-shirts and Update Master Guest List – week three

At this time, you can also order the commemorative T-shirts. Souvenir T-shirts are a big part of many AG events. Our grads and guests indicate their shirt size on their agreements, but you can simply have a supply of varied sizes on hand once you have an idea of group size. We order plain white T-shirts each year and provide them along with fabric or permanent markers. The signing of shirts often takes place just after arrival and can last more than an hour. Our grads tell us it's one of their favourite activities at the event, and serves as a permanent reminder of a great time and the great friendships they have made in high school.

If you are working with guest sizes from Agreements, you can enter the T-shirt sizes on the Master Guest List, and then use this as your sign out sheet on the night of the event. If you are ordering bulk for the event, you will only need to keep a list of the various sizes you ordered, rather than names.

Follow Up on Supplier Invoices, Order payments – week four

Hopefully you have received a few invoices by now. If not, you can follow up and remind suppliers that you can't pay them until you have an approved invoice in your hands. Your sub-committee will need to check the invoice for accuracy before forwarding it on to your finance coordinator who will arrange for payment. Payments will be made at various times; some during daytime installation, some entertainers on event night, and others will be paid immediately following the event. Either way, the more invoices you have in your hands, the faster those payments can be made – you don't want to be paying out invoices in July, long after schools are closed and committee members are on vacation. It's a good thing for each committee to keep track of their own suppliers since you have built that relationship, rather than having the finance coordinator try to track them down, weeks later.

 FUNDRAISING & PRIZES

Create and Distribute Supplier Agreements – week one

This committee may not require Supplier Agreements as you are working mainly with donations and immediate purchases. If you do have an agreement with a company or organization for a number of prize items or for any reason feel it would be worthwhile to have an agreement, you can modify the form to suit.

Included in the Agreement are the terms for payment. Ask for an invoice complete with all contact information pricing including all taxes. Give suppliers two weeks and then in week four you can follow up. You may have companies that are invoicing for prizes, so this may be a worthwhile step for your group.

The sample "Supplier Agreement" is available in Appendix – Forms and as a PDF document or as a Word document at www.safegradevent.com/tools/forms/supplieragreement

Develop Prize Budget and Allocation List – week two

Depending on how many fundraising dollars you have raised on behalf of the prize draw, you may be able to start putting together your Prize Budget and develop a Prize List. Each year we poll our grad class to see what types of prizes are "in" for that year, as they often have very definite ideas of what they would like to win. Times change fast in the world of teens, so the cell phones we gave away in 2006 held no appeal in 2010 when iPhones were much more popular and everyone already had the latest standard cell. Our goal has been to provide at least one prize for every grad in attendance (we do not provide prizes for guests), and the prizes range from a $20.00 gas or coffee card to a laptop computer. Each year we set aside a separate prize for the casino winner (the grad who accumulates the most 'faux' wealth), another prize for the bingo and contest winners (we put all the names of those who won games throughout the event, in a hat and select a winner). We also solicit local businesses, and have provided three to five bursaries each year for those who are moving on to post secondary education. Remember to include in your prize budget any of the items that are being used at the After-Grad and then given away, as these will come out of your budget. We use prize funds to purchase our foosball, air hockey, *Nintendo XBOX* and *Wii* games that we include in our lounge/games room each year, and then those are given away at the end of the night.

Some AG events include winning a car in their draw, and it can be a fabulous and exciting grand prize. Some groups have a car donated by a local dealer, or they have someone knowledgeable purchase a used car, and then local automotive suppliers donate products and services to make improvements. At our first After-Grad, we were lucky enough to have a parent in the automotive industry purchase a car and generously give of their time to refurbish it, resulting in a wonderful grand prize. We unveiled our car at our school's May Grad Breakfast launch, but some groups keep the actual car a secret until it's won and then it's unveiled following the event, at the school – to a big fanfare!

Once you have developed a budget and allocated amounts to particular prizes, you will have a good idea of how much more you need in the way of funding or how flush you are, and you can increase the value of the some of the prizes. You will need some shoppers to go out and purchase the prizes, and we usually do this in the first week of June. At the event, we put all of the grad names (from our Master Guest List) into a raffle drum for the draw.

Follow Up on Supplier Invoices and Order Payments – week four

As mentioned earlier, you may not have many supplier invoices to gather, but if you do, now is the time to send out reminders. Your sub-committee will need to check the invoice for accuracy before forwarding it on to your finance coordinator who will arrange for payment. The faster you have the invoices in your hands, the faster those payments can be made – you don't want to be paying out invoices in July, long after schools are closed and committee members are on vacation. It's a good thing for each sub-committee to keep track of their own suppliers since you have built that relationship, rather than making the finance coordinator try to track them down, weeks later.

 AG Committee Meeting and Thank-Yous – week four

This may be your last or second last meeting before the actual event, so it should be used to tie up any loose ends and for every sub-committee to touch base and to ask for help or support if needed. Most will be feeling good at this point, under control, and if you are lucky, you will still have much of June to complete outstanding items.

I have always been a fan of handwritten thank-you cards to suppliers, however, I realize that times have changed and it is not necessary nor good for the environment to be using additional paper and cards, so I understand if you choose another method to say thanks, such as email. It is important however, to acknowledge the support you have received for the event, and it makes sense to get that thank-you list ready and even write the template now, while you still have time and energy. After the event, you will be physically and emotionally tired, so write them now.

Committees should each be responsible for their own specific Thank-Yous, having built their own relationships, but using a template for a consistent and unified look and one that represents your school/society with the school logo or colours, is best.

I include in my thank-you a note about the event's success and a reminder of why we do the event. I also ask if we can count on their inclusion and/or support for the upcoming year, and I provide the date if I can, so they can mark their calendars.

The website and newspaper Thank-Yous are usually of a more general nature than those sent to suppliers and this may take a group effort to send the desired message. The Thank-You to be included on the school/society website and/or a local newspaper, will likely be a blanket thanks to the community you are addressing and should recognize the support of the business community, local service organizations, the school administration, parents, etc. It's important to use this time to remind people of the tremendous importance of a safe After-Grad and to commend those willing to show support.

> *"It brings the whole grad class together in a fun way. It was a great way to celebrate, a great way to end high school. I have great memories from that night because I wasn't drunk."*
>
> — Andrew, graduate

JUNE

June, it's finally here – let the event begin! What an exciting and wonderful time for graduates and for your team as you put all those months of hard work into action and watch this group of amazing young men and women graduate and share their very best school memories at their After-Grad.

Because your After-Grad may happen in any week this month, I have set up this section of the book into pre-event, event, and post-event activities. And, depending on your event date, your debriefing meeting may happen sometime this month or may have to wait until September. Regardless of your event date, you will need to complete all of the tasks listed to operate a successful event.

JUNE – ACTION ITEMS

Week	Chair	Communications & Publicity Co-ordinator	Finances Co-ordinator	Volunteer Committee	Transportation, Operations & Safety Committee	Decorating, Food & Beverage Committee	Entertainment, Games & Contests Committee	Fundraising & Prizes Committee
Pre Event	Complete the AG Binder	Write the Bus Escort Script	Write 'onsite' supplier cheques	Distribute Event Info Email	Reconfirm & Walk Through with Wellness & Security Teams	Guarantee F&B Order	Distribute "Event Schedule" to Venue	Purchase Prizes
							Touch Base Supplier Phone Call	

THE AFTER-GRAD EVENT

Post Event	AG Committee Debrief Meeting	AG Committee Debrief Meeting	AG Committee Debrief Meeting	AG Committee Debrief Meeting	AG Committee Debrief Meeting	AG Committee Debrief Meeting	AG Committee Debrief Meeting	AG Committee Debrief Meeting
	Distribute Thank-Yous & Gifts		Pay Invoices & Complete Budget Analysis					

Sample "Action Items – June" is available in Appendix – Forms and as a PDF document or as an Excel document at www.safegradevent.com/tools/forms/actionitemsjune

PRE EVENT

 ## CHAIR

Complete the AG binder

You can now complete the AG binder that was created in April when the Agreements were received. This binder is now reviewed to make sure that every form is indeed complete, has all the necessary and appropriate signatures, along with any medical information. This is your final opportunity to secure missing information prior to the event.

It's a good idea to review your binder and your Master Guest List with the school administrators to be sure everyone is on the same page; they know the students.

Cross-reference your binder with the Master Guest List and make the following notations:

- ✓ Cross-reference to identify those attending the dinner/dance only (the school will have their own list for this event) as you <u>will not</u> be transferring them to the After-Grad. Include this information in the "notes section" beside that grad's name.
- ✓ Mark an "x" in the "Medical Alert" section to assist the wellness team in identifying individuals for whom they may need additional information. This information will be found in the AG Binder – this should be done by the chair of the AG Committee, for consistency of confidentiality. Be sure to keep this master copy of the list separate from any others, so that the medical alerts are not shared with anyone else until the event. When printing off other copies of the "check off" list, you can simply take off the medical alert information prior to sharing by email or printing from your Excel sheet.
- ✓ Add any additional "Exit" alert information or instructions as per the completed forms, noting any changes since April along with any important notes for reference at the event (this may include early departures, parental notes).

The AG Binder travels with the chair to the event and must be kept confidential, allowing access only to the onsite wellness or security teams, or school administrators.

COMMUNICATIONS & PUBLICITY

Write the Bus Escort Script

If you are transferring your group by bus to the venue, you have the perfect opportunity to create some excitement and anticipation and to let the group know just what's in store for them at the event. Signage at the event will also provide information, but we have found that many of the grads and guests are too excited or overwhelmed to read the signs once they arrive.

We try to theme our bus script each year and we include as much information as possible. You have a captive audience and a microphone, so make of use it.

A sample "Bus Script" is available in Appendix – Forms and as a PDF document or as a Word document at www.safegradevent.com/tools/forms/busscript

FINANCE

Write "Onsite" Supplier Cheques

While some suppliers will invoice you following the event, others may require payment onsite on the day/night of the event. Some will want to be paid when they install earlier that day (rental companies) and some will want to be paid immediately following their performance (bands, magicians etc.). The chair can distribute all cheques if he/she is onsite or can delegate to the volunteer handling the daytime installation, or to the entertainment sub-committee leader. Prior to issuing any cheques, be sure you have an invoice from the supplier that can be marked "paid". You must have the proper paper invoice documentation to match all payments.

# VOLUNTEERS

Distribute Event Info Email

This may be the last time to connect with volunteers prior to the actual event, so it's important to send out any pertinent event information. In an effort to keep the printing to a minimum we try to email as much as possible. We send out an Information Email & Volunteer Grid to all volunteers a few days ahead of the event. For those in a lead position or supervisory role, I also include an Event Schedule – for example, the lead person in the coat check, room supervisors, and the lead person on the decor team. It's not necessary for everyone volunteering to have the event schedule, as it may be a lengthy document and appear daunting, and we don't want to scare off volunteers. Limited copies of the schedule are available at the event for reference.

We include the following information in our email:
- ✓ arrival & briefing time and location for all volunteers
- ✓ a map of the venue location, directions for driving/carpooling, public transit
- ✓ venue parking availability and associated costs with a recommendation that volunteers not drive, but make alternate morning pickup arrangements as they too will have been awake almost 24 hours and it may be unsafe for them to drive
- ✓ security information including the entrance procedures (volunteers are subject to the same security measures as attendees), and wellness team information
- ✓ what to wear, what to bring (this may be related to a theme, costumes, etc.)
- ✓ food & beverage details/restrictions for volunteers – what is/isn't being provided
- ✓ a respectful request that although it's a day of celebration, adult volunteers recog-

nize that the event is "dry" and that they use discretion around consuming alcohol prior to assisting at the event.

TRANSPORTATION, OPERATIONS, & SAFETY

Reconfirm & Walk Through with Wellness & Security Teams

It's important to review with both your wellness and security teams, your expectations for the event along with everyone's responsibilities. We provide a list of items that are not permitted at our event, and the security team explains in detail their entrance procedure. We augment the paid security team with our own volunteers (we ask for parents who may be police officers, firefighters, security/customs officers in their daily lives and are familiar with this type of procedure). It's important to work together as one team. Some of our "security policies" include:

- ✓ While our grads/guests sign "Agreements" to stay for the duration of the night, for those who do leave prior to the end, we do not offer in/out privileges – if the grad/guest leaves the event at any time, they are not be permitted to return.
- ✓ Guests undergo a "pat down" by the same gender security officer, and all pockets are searched. Any additional items including purses, change of clothes bags, etc., are also searched and "checked" into the supervised coat check.
- ✓ Anyone suspected of having used alcohol or drugs prior to entrance may be subject to a breathalyser or may be refused admittance – a paid police officer is onsite to administer the breathalyser and/or escort the individual to a waiting area while parents/guardians are contacted.
- ✓ All grads/guests must provide a contact name and phone number in case a parent/guardian needs to be contacted during the event.
- ✓ No liquids are permitted to be brought into the venue. This includes bottled water – as we provide that at the event.

- ✓ All medication (unless it is required during the event and must be on their person) is handed over to the doctor on the wellness team to be kept until needed. The doctor also has a number of over-the-counter remedies on hand for situations including headaches, upset stomachs, etc. that can be provided if necessary. Medical protocol is followed and guests are responsible to self-administer their own medication under the supervision of the onsite doctor or nurses inside the Wellness Room.
- ✓ Purses are handed over and remain at the coat check where guests may have unlimited access to the purse contents, however, they are not permitted to take that purse into the event.
- ✓ Cell phones and digital cameras are permitted and may be left at the Coat Check with unlimited access.

DECORATING, FOOD & BEVERAGE

Guarantee F&B order

You provided your order earlier, but you may now need to provide a guarantee for the Food & Beverage. This will have been clearly stated in any contracts you may have signed. You can underestimate and suppliers will ensure that they have extra food on hand. If there is a facility to make additional supplies and if numbers unexpectedly increase, then you can usually have more food made. Remember you will be charged for the guaranteed amounts, so be conservative.

ENTERTAINMENT, GAMES, CONTESTS

Distribute Event Schedule to Venue

Email the Event Schedule to your venue contact so he/she can review it and advise of any incorrect or missing information. It's always helpful to have a fresh set of eyes review your documents, especially since you have been looking at them for so long, it's easy to miss things. It also shows the venue that you are organized and installs confidence in their team that everything is under control... and it is!

Touch Base Supplier Phone Call

Because entertainment is so important to the success of the After-Grad, we make a phone call to each entertainer, performer or supplier a few days before the event to touch base. As event planners, we need to be sure that as much as possible, everything will go according to plan – then we are ready to react to any challenges or situations that always come up (always) on the night of the event, knowing our partners are ready to go.

 # FUNDRAISING & PRIZES

Purchase Prizes

It's time to go shopping – who knew this committee could be so much fun! You will need to purchase all of the gift cards and smaller prizes to have at the event, but you may decide to keep the larger items at the store or at the school until after the event. It may be easier to keep expensive and/or larger items away from the event site, especially if the winners are traveling home by bus – it is hard to take a 32-inch TV onboard.

"Dry After-Grads set a good example to let kids know that as parents we support dry parties—you don't need to get high on alcohol or drugs to have a great time. It is fun activities, friends, laughter, and good times that make special memories."

— Cheryl, parent volunteer

THE AFTERGRAD EVENT

Because committees may be involved in several different areas within the event, this section of the book has been set up to follow the flow of the event rather than by committee. Follow your Event Schedule, trust your volunteer team to do their job, and enjoy the night!

Daytime Installations & Set Up

If all goes according to plan, your Installation Schedule will be the guide for the venue and your volunteer in charge of receiving deliveries and suppliers today. Make sure you have a couple of contact names and numbers available in case of emergency but you should anticipate smooth sailing, since you have your system in place.

Evening Volunteer Briefing – one and half to three hours prior to the event

With all of your volunteers gathered together, take the time to do a briefing prior to the event start. This is the time to review the Event Schedule, to answer questions, and to complete the event set-up.

We generally set up tables in our Wellness/Volunteer Room with all of the components needed for each area/room, along with a floor plan of that room, set-up instructions and a table checklist. This allows volunteers to get started right way following the briefing, there are fewer questions, and time is used efficiently. We keep our set-up area organized and clean so that later on during the teardown, we can return items to those same tables prior to packing up. Use checklists to make sure everything makes it back to your central set-up area. Remember that volunteers will be much more tired at the end of the event, having been up for almost 24 hours, so make it easy for everyone and they won't have to think quite so hard. Each table in our set-up area is marked with a room/area name. We include tables for Transportation, Outdoor Entrance, Main concourse, Casino, Games Room, Nightclub, and Wellness/Volunteers. Our table lists might include:

TRANSPORTATION TABLE – wristbands, Master Guest List, radios, garbage/recycling bags, colour bus signs (to match the wristband colours)

OUTDOOR ENTRANCE – palm trees, archway, carpet and stanchions, lighting, grad sign, extension cords and power bars, outdoor clothing

MAIN CONCOURSE – Security supplies (small storage bags, labels, markers), buffet linens and decorations, popcorn machine and supplies, T-shirts, serving trays, washroom amenities, Coat Check supplies

CASINO – bingo game and supplies, buffet linens and decorations, casino bucks, dealer red pens (so no one can alter their numbers except the dealers), dealer costumes

GAMES ROOM – buffet linens and decorations, board games, video game systems/games, limbo & hula hoop contest props

NIGHTCLUB – Prize Draw raffle drum, buffet linens and decorations, beach balls, glow sticks, tea light holders & candles

WELLNESS & VOLUNTEERS – event toolbox (scissors, various kinds of tape, fishing line for hanging signs, string, twist ties, extra labels) , volunteer costumes, Doctor's Alert List, mats, linens, medical supplies.

Transportation to the Event

With everything in hand, you have what you need to ensure this part of the event runs smoothly. If you are not transferring guests, you will make the call to open the doors and let the first guests make their way through registration and security. Or, like our group, you may have one team at the AG venue handling last minute decorating, while another team is at the dinner/dance location, getting ready to transfer guests.

Your Master Guest List will identify who should receive a wristband and board a bus and once you have everyone on board, your volunteers can read their script along the way. Upon arrival at the venue, just give the bus a quick check to make sure no one has left any personal belongings on board, and all extra novelties are picked up and taken into the event.

Arrival and Security Check

When guests arrive, we leave the security check-in to the professionals. This is a very important component of the event, and in order to ensure a safe and secure event, you need to let the security firm or parent security team do their job. With additional volunteer parents there to assist, the main focus at this time is that guests arrive both alcohol and drug free, and that their personal belongings are checked thoroughly before entering the building. Storage bags can be used for medications to be held by the doctor, and other small items to be stored at the coat check and extra garment bags and drycleaner bags (donated) can be used to store suits and gowns as guests change.

Once through the security line, guests are ready to enjoy themselves, and they can now enjoy a welcome mocktail, and get busy having fun!

The Middle of the Night

As you move through the night, you will find that the Event Schedule is all your committee team needs to operate the event. Because you have all taken the time and put in the hours of work necessary, the night will unfold as it should, in an organized manner. You will be able to react to any situations that arise during the night, and emerge in the morning, a tired and very satisfied group!

Prize Draw and the Ride Home

Our event culminates, usually at about four am, with an exciting prize draw which brings the entire group back together in one space, and serves as a great finale to a wonderful event. We give out the first round of prizes, one to every grad in attendance, which gives everyone a taste for winning. Following that, we pull the names for the other prizes including electronics, computers and the larger ticket items. The bursaries and tuitions, and maybe a car, are the last prizes announced. Once everyone has something in their hands, the group can make their way back to the coat check to pick up any personal belongings, and then into the line up for pickup or the return ride home.

If you have parents picking up, you will need to have your lists ready for sign out so you can be sure that everyone connects with a driver. If you are using buses, you can send your grads out to a bus that matches their wristband colour. Buses can leave as soon as they have their whole group, and their volunteer escorts. Before the last bus leaves, be sure that you have checked the venue, including washrooms, for any leftover guests – you don't want to leave anyone behind!

Once the group is out of the building and safely on their way, you can do any additional tearing down or clean up that is necessary, making sure that all rentals are stored together to make it easier for suppliers to pick up later that day. Now you can all go home and get some much deserved rest, knowing that you kept the grad class safe and gave them a night they will always remember – a truly unforgettable After-Grad!

> *"My After-Grad was one of the most amazing, memorable nights of my life. Bringing the whole grad class together for an awesome party is really unforgettable."*
>
> — Callum, graduate

POST EVENT

 ## AG Committee Debrief Meeting

With months of planning and a very successful event finally over, the last thing you will want to talk about now is the After-Grad! But, this is an important meeting, and it's always a good idea to have a debrief or a review while the event is still fresh in your mind. If your event was held in the last week of June, you may need to wait until September to review, but do ask your committee chairs to write their debrief notes now, while they can still remember this event, and while the parents are still affiliated with the school, as for some, this may be their final year.

Use this time to record your successes and your challenges, and to give next year's committee a starting point. Make suggestions for positive change, and remember to celebrate what went well, the areas where you wouldn't change a thing.

And, if you have some energy left, tell them what you thought about the event, from a parent's point of view – how it felt to be a part of such an important and exciting night, to watch the graduating class, and maybe even your own son or daughter, make memories that will last a lifetime, in a safe, secure environment. That feeling is priceless, so pass it on!!!

Distribute Thank-Yous & Gifts

Whether you are publicly thanking in a newspaper ad, or on a website, or privately thanking by email or thank-you card, it's important that these be sent promptly following the event. Everyone is tired, but it's essential to thank those who have supported your efforts. Review your lists once again for accuracy to ensure that you have not forgotten anyone. All committees need to consult on this so that every thank-you is accounted for and there is no overlap. Keep this list for next year's committee as this will give them a starting point for their support appeals. As well, gifts need to be distributed at this time.

Pay Invoices & Complete Budget Analysis – Finance Coordinator and Chair

You will have already paid some invoices – those who required payment on the day/ night of the event. Putting your Budget Analysis together will provide a list of suppliers, and you can use that list to follow up on any outstanding payments. And if your school is assisting you with payments, remind suppliers that the schools shut down for a period during the summer, so they need to send in those invoices immediately. File your invoices in alpha order by supplier name to match the Budget Analysis that is sorted the same way. It is especially important to keep accurate and organized records for an event this size.

Sample "Budget Analysis" is available in Appendix – Forms and as a PDF document or as an Excel document at www.safegradevent.com/tools/forms/budgetanalysis

> *"There is so much to do that you don't feel like you need alcohol to make it fun."*
>
> — Jason, graduate

APPENDIX

FORMS

All Forms are listed in this section in the order in which they first appear in the book. They, along with the monthly Action Item Calendars (see page references below), are also available for downloading on the website – www.safegradevent.com in PDF format or as Word or Excel documents.

ACTION ITEM CALENDARS	page		page
September	18	February	80
October	24	March	88
November	34	April	100
December	74	May	110
January	76	June	130

FORMS		page			page
Volunteer Form	Sept.	146	Grad Attendance Agreement	Feb.	162
Venue Questions	Oct.	147	Guest Attendance Agreement	Feb.	164
Event Flow	Nov.	149	Event Schedule	March	166
Survey	Nov.	150	Volunteer Grid	March	172
Survey Report	Nov.	151	Installation Schedule	March	175
Quote Sheet	Nov.	152	Floor Plan	April	176
Supplier Contact List	Nov.	153	Master Attendance List	May	177
Event Budget	Nov.	154	Master Guest List	May	178
Supplier Questions	Nov.	157	Supplier Agreement	May	179
Food Provider Questions	Nov.	158	Food & Beverage Order	May	180
Performer Questions	Nov.	159	Performer Agreement	May	181
Prize Solicitation Letter	Nov.	160	Bus Escort Script	June	182
Tuition Solicitation Letter	Nov.	161	Budget Analysis	June	183

VOLUNTEER FORM – SEPTEMBER

SCHOOL or GRAD LOGO

AFTERGRAD VOLUNTEER FORM

Hello, parents of grade 12 graduates. We would like to organize an all night safe, dry After-Grad event following the school sponsored grad activities in (month). We are planning an exciting & unforgettable event and we will need the help of many volunteers.

You can help us create an After-Grad committee. Please indicate below, any areas of interest. If you can also help us out at the actual event, please indicate this in the space provided.

Committee Chair (position) _____   Communications & Publicity (position) ____

Finance Coordinator (position) _____   Volunteer Sub-committee _____

Transportation, Operations & Safety _____   Decorating, Food & Beverage _____
(Sub-committee)   (Sub-committee)

Entertainment, Games & Contests _____   Fundraising & Prizes _____
(Sub-committee)   (Sub- committee)

The After-Grad – helping out at the actual event   _____

Please note that even if you are not interested or able to help out in one of the areas listed above, we would appreciate you filing in your contact information. We want to keep everyone informed about the event, throughout the grad year.

Graduating student's name: _____

Parent/volunteer name: _____

Parent/volunteer name: _____

Daytime phone #:   _____

Evening phone #:   _____

Email address: _____

Secondary Email address: _____

http://www.safegradevent.com/tools/forms/volunteer

VENUE QUESTIONS – OCTOBER

VENUE QUESTIONS

GENERAL RULES & GUIDELINES

- How large is the overall space and smaller function spaces -can it accommodate our group size? Review spaces with "air walls" that can be divided into smaller spaces

- Are there any spaces that would serve as "rain backup" if the weather does not cooperate? This will affect registration/entrance as well as any outdoor games/activities (inflatables)

- May we include any outdoor spaces as part of the event and if so, is there a way to enclose those spaces, such as perimeter fencing. Can the venue provide a perimeter?

- What parking is available, and are there any associated costs?

- Is the venue wheelchair accessible?

- Are there any bylaws/rules or restrictions that we need to be aware of such as surrounding traffic, parking, noise, and can we control access or man all entrances and exits?

- How late can the event go? Sometimes additional charges apply to late night/early am events

- Are there any exclusive or preferred supplier contracts? For example, some venues have a list of preferred suppliers or hold exclusive contracts with suppliers including caterers, audio visual (sound & lighting) or security firms and you must use those suppliers for your event

- Are there any rules/restrictions on what can and cannot be brought into the venue, including food & beverage (items such as bottled water can be very expensive to purchase from venue/ caterer, providing your own can save in cost), candles with open flames, etc.

- Does the venue have storage and/or refrigeration facilities that can be used for incoming items, and can items be brought in prior to the event date if required?

- What coverage is supplied under your venue insurance, and what additional event or liability insurance do we need to secure? Ask for a copy of their insurance or a written certificate outlining what is/isn't covered – offer to provide your event liability or society insurance certificate once it's available

- Are there any rules about rigging or hanging signage, decorations, taping walls, dropping balloons or scattering confetti?

- Are there any additional permits we need to provide?

FACILITY & AMENITIES

- Is there wireless available in all or any of the spaces?

- Is there an existing stage and/or dance floor, or do we need to provide them?

- Are there additional rooms that might be used for volunteers, wellness &rest, performers/suppliers, and can this be included in the price of the venue space?

http://www.safegradevent.com/tools/forms/venuequestions   ... / page 2

VENUE QUESTIONS (cont'd) – OCTOBER

- Is there an existing sound system and in what space (s) is it available? There may be a number of activities going on simultaneously, so sound overlap is a consideration
- Is there any existing seating/tables, if not, how many dining/buffet tables can be accommodated and in what spaces?
- What washroom, coat check, garbage and recycling facilities are available?
- What is in place for first aid, evacuation/emergency plans etc.

CONTRACTS & COSTS

- Will you be personally handling our event? If not, who will be our main contact person, what is their direct contact information, including a cell phone number?
- May we see a copy of your standard contract?
- What is the rental cost for the venue and are there any other additional costs associated with rental. What is included in the rental fee, what is not included?
- Are there any complimentary products/services included in the contract or available at no extra charge? Some venues stock a limited supply of linens, or have an onsite sound & lighting technician. Some activities & rentals such as swimming, and hockey/tennis equipment in a leisure centre may be included with a venue rental.
- Are there additional fees, including janitorial or cleaning costs, SOCAN fees (music licensing), staff overtime charges if the event runs over the scheduled time?
- Do you require a deposit in order to hold the date for our event, and if so, how much of a deposit and when is it due? When would the balance owing be due? What is your cancellation policy?
- Is there a discount applicable if we pay by cash or cheque, rather than by credit card?

Try to provide the following event details to the venue; it will assist them in quoting:

- The event date/timing
- The group size (the size of grad class plus 10-15% extra for guests)
- The approximate number of onsite volunteers and suppliers (allow 25-30 for a group of 200, or 15% of the total guest number)

http://www.safegradevent.com/tools/forms/venuequestions

EVENT FLOW – NOVEMBER

AFTER-GRAD EVENT FLOW
"PARKLAND PARADISE"

TIMING	ROOM/AREA	ACTIVITY/EVENT
10.30 – 11.00 pm	Transfer to After-Grad	Buses & Escorts, Novelties, Security, Coat Check
10.45 – 2 am	Nightclub	DJ, Dancing, Dance Contests
10.45 pm – 3 am	Main Concourse	T-Shirts, Tattoo Artists, Magician, Caricaturists, Hot Dog & Popcorn vendors, Pizza Kiosk, Rock Band, DDR, Beach Relay
10.45 pm – 3 am	Games Room/Lounge	Karaoke, Photo Loop, Video Games, Arcade Games, Air Hockey, Foosball, Photo booth, Contests (Limbo & Hula)
10.45 – 3.30 am	Casino	Poker, Blackjack, Wheel, Billiards, Bingo
10.45 – 4.30 am	All rooms	Buffets - Veggies, Snacks, Dessert items, Granola Bars, Fresh Fruit, Bottled Water, Soft drinks, Coffee
2.00 – 2.30 am	Nightclub	Live Band performance
2.30 – 4.00 am	Nightclub	Hypnotist performance
4.00 am	Nightclub	Grad Prize Draw
4.45 - 5.00 am	Main Concourse	Coat check, sign out & bus transfer home
5.30 am	Sidney – Beacon Plaza	Bus arrival, Parent pick up

http://www.safegradevent.com/tools/forms/eventflow

SURVEY – NOVEMBER

SCHOOL or GRAD LOGO
AFTER-GRAD (YEAR) SURVEY

School name is proud to announce its 5th annual all night After-Grad at venue location on **date and time** (following the School sponsored graduation ceremony & dinner/dance) The parent After-Grad committee along with the student grad executive wants this to be an exciting and memorable event and you can help create your very best After-Grad by completing this survey.

Please select 2 possible themes from the suggestions below or provide your own suggestion:

Viva Las Vegas ____ Around the World ____ Glitz n Glamour ____ The Red Carpet/Hollywood ____
Tropical ____ Black & White ____ Mardi gras ____ Masquerade ____ Jungle/Safari ____
Movies n Musicals ____ Nautical ____ Sand n Surf/Beach ____ Winter Wonderland ____

Some of the activities we may include are:
- Casino games, including blackjack, poker, billiards, bingo
- A nightclub with dancing , dance contests, music videos
- A live performance by a hypnotist/comedian
- Interactive entertainment such as magicians, caricature artists, airbrush tattoos, t-shirt signing
- A games room & lounge with arcade & video games, karaoke, a photo booth and much more
- All night buffets with fresh, hot pizza, hotdogs, popcorn, finger foods, snacks, and beverages

This is your chance to have your say, so please take the time to let us know how to create the best ever After-Grad!

Any other casino games you would like to include? _____

Do you want the DJ to offer dance contests, song requests, music videos? _____

Would you like to include a live band performance? _____ Suggested band? _____

What other entertainment would you like to include? _____

Which arcade games would you like to play? _____

Which video games would you like to play? _____

Do you want Foosball? _____ Air Hockey? _____ Any other games? _____

Would you like us to show a movie, sports event etc. on a TV or screen? _____

What foods would you like to see on the buffet? _____

Any other suggestions or comments: _____

_____

Grad name: _____

Note: The After-Grad is a school supported, not a school sponsored event, and **Attendance Agreements & parental consent are required for participation. Please return** this form to the school office or a grad exec member by **November 6th. THANKS!**

http://www.safegradevent.com/tools/forms/survey

SURVEY REPORT - NOVEMBER

AFTER-GRAD SURVEY REPORT			
SURVEY QUESTION	**1st CHOICE**	**2nd CHOICE**	**NOTES**
Theme suggestion	Black & White	Jungle/Safari	
Any other casino games you would like to include?	Bingo-22 Yes		Bingo will also be offered this year in the Casino
Do you want the DJ to offer dance contests, song requests, music videos?	Contests & Spot Dances - 45		Will request some contests and spot dances from the DJ
Would you like to include a live band performance, suggested band?	49 Yes, 18 No		We will invite the local band "Couch:85" to play for a half hour
What other entertainment would you like to include?	Laser Tag		Can't accommodate - venue space restrictions & safety regulations
	Limbo Game		This will be included along with some other fun "tropical" contests - with prizes
	Mini Golf		Can't accommodate - venue space restrictions & safety regulations
Which arcade games would you like to play?	Pac man - 34	Pinball - 15	Both are available and may be rented for the event
Which video games would you like to play?	Rock band - 12	Guitar Hero - 9 Halo - 8	All are available and all 3 will be included in the event
Do you want Foosball, Air Hockey, any other games?	Foosball - 66	Air Hockey- 63	Will have both at the event. Pool/billiards was also requested, see below
Would you like us to show a movie, sports event etc. or on a TV or screen	Yes - 53		There will be music videos playing in the nightclub, and we will add a movie to fit the theme
What foods would you like to see on the buffet?			Pita and hummus, veggies & dip, potato chips, sandwiches, brownies
Any other suggestions or comments ?	Pool Table - 29		Pool had the most votes in this category - If budget & space allow, we will rent a pool table for the event
	TWISTER		We will include TWISTER in the Games Room

http://www.safegradevent.com/tools/forms/surveyrreport

QUOTE SHEET – NOVEMBER

AFTER-GRAD QUOTE SHEET (budget area)						
Supplier Name	#	Unit Cost	Sub Total	PST/ GST/ HST	Total	Notes
Number of Guests	200					
DJ Services - Nightclub	1	$ 1,000.00	$ 1,000.00	$ 120.00	$ 1,120.00	Cost includes Sound & Light package
Hypnotist/Comedian - 90 min show	1	$ 2,000.00	$ 2,000.00	$ 240.00	$ 2,240.00	Requires bottled water, 24 chairs onstage, mic
Magician - 4 hr call	1	$ 500.00	$ 500.00	$ 60.00	$ 560.00	Main Concourse
Caricaturist - 4 hr call	2	$ 400.00	$ 800.00	$ 96.00	$ 896.00	
Tattoo Artist - All Colours Inc. - 4 hr. call	1	$ 500.00	$ 500.00	$ 60.00	$ 560.00	Requires deposit & signed contract
Photo Booth - 4 hr. Call	1	$ 1,250.00	$ 1,250.00	$ 150.00	$ 1,400.00	Includes attendant, set up & teardown
T-Shirts	1	$ 500.00	$ 500.00	$ 60.00	$ 560.00	White, no logo
Photo Loop Screen Rental	1	$ 25.00	$ 25.00	$ 3.00	$ 28.00	Rental from venue
Arcade Games Rental	1	$ 750.00	$ 750.00	$ 90.00	$ 840.00	Pinball, Pac Man
Pool Table Rental	1	$ 525.00	$ 525.00	$ 63.00	$ 588.00	Incl set up/teardown
Foosball, Air Hockey	1	$ -	$ -	$ -	$ -	per survey results, prize budget
AV - TVs, DVDs, Screens	1	$ 800.00	$ 800.00	$ 96.00	$ 896.00	
Video Games	1	$ -	$ -	$ -	$ -	per survey results, prize budget
Bingo Sound System	1	$ 200.00	$ 200.00	$ 24.00	$ 224.00	Rental from venue
Bingo Game	1	$ -	$ -	$ -	$ -	Corporate donation
Casino Game Rentals	1	$ 1,250.00	$ 1,250.00	$ 150.00	$ 1,400.00	Includes blackjack, wheel, poker
Raffle Drum rental	1	$ 20.00	$ 20.00	$ 2.40	$ 22.40	Incl dlvry, pickup
Contests & Prizes	1	$ 150.00	$ 150.00	$ 18.00	$ 168.00	Props, novelties
Total - Entertainment, Games & Contests					$ 11,502.40	
Contact Information:		Name:	John Merling		Phone:	250-656-000
Vegas Casino Rentals		Onsite Cell:	250-888-0000	Web:	www.vegascasinorentals.ca	
		Email:	info@vegascasinorentals.com			
Taxes may differ from province to province, and year to year						

http://www.safegradevent.com/tools/forms/quotesheet

SUPPLIER CONTACT LIST – NOVEMBER

AFTER-GRAD SUPPLIER CONTACT LIST							
Co Name	Product Service	Last Name	First Name	Office Phone	Email	Onsite Cell	Address
Vegas Casino Rentals	Casino Games	Merling	John	250 656 0000	info@vegascasinorentals.com	250 888 0000	497 Shoreview Road, Victoria, BC V9L 2S6

http://www.safegradevent.com/tools/forms/suppliercontact

EVENT BUDGET – NOVEMBER

AFTER-GRAD EVENT BUDGET (at date)					
Carryover from previous year's After-Grad		$0.00			
Projected ticket sales - based on $90.00 per x 200		$18,000.00			
PAC donation		$1,500.00			
Income from local town council		$1,250.00			
Fundraising – bottle drive campaign		$1,800.00			
Fundraising – grocery cards campaign		$1,500.00			
Private donations		$2,200.00			
TOTAL PROJECTED STARTING INCOME		**$26,250.00**			
ITEM DESCRIPTION	#	COST	SUB TOTAL	PST/ GST/ HST	TOTAL	%
TRANSPORTATION (5-7%)						
double decker shuttle -dinner/dance to AG venue	1	$ 600.00	$ 600.00	$ 72.00	$ 672.00	
Bus return transfer to the town centre	1	$ 800.00	$ 800.00	$ 96.00	$ 896.00	
					$ 1,568.00	6%
OPERATIONS & SECURITY (18-20%)						
Venue rental - includes security, janitorial, SOCAN fees	1	$3,700.00	$ 3,700.00	$444.00	$ 4,144.00	
Event/liability Insurance	1	$ 200.00	$ 200.00	$ 24.00	$ 224.00	
ID Wristbands - internet purchase	1	$ 50.00	$ 50.00	$ 6.00	$ 56.00	
Flashlights for bus loading, clothing handout (donated)	1	$ -	$ -	$ -	$ -	
Privacy screens for wellness room - venue rental	4	$ 15.00	$ 60.00	$ 7.20	$ 67.20	
Wellness room supplies - meds/first aid supplies	1	$ 50.00	$ 50.00	$ 6.00	$ 56.00	
School first aid kit - on loan for the event	1	$ -	$ -	$ -	$ -	
Coat check tags - donated by local business	1	$ -	$ -	$ -	$ -	
Radios for onsite coordinators - 4 Supervisors	4	$ 35.00	$ 140.00	$ 16.80	$ 156.80	
Washroom amenities	1	$ 100.00	$ 100.00	$ 12.00	$ 112.00	
					$ 4,816.00	18%

cont'd...

http://safegradevent.com/tools/forms/eventbudget

EVENT BUDGET (con't) – NOVEMBER

AFTER-GRAD EVENT BUDGET (at date)						
ITEM DESCRIPTION	#	COST	SUB	HST	TOTAL	%
DECORATIONS (10%)						
Grad and volunteer novelty Items	1	$ 325.00	$ 325.00	$ 39.00	$ 364.00	
Flashing welcome sign (donated)	1	$ -	$ -	$ -	$ -	
Red carpet, stanchions, ropes, rope lighting, install and year Down (50', 12 posts, 10 ropes)	1	$ 313.80	$ 313.80	$ 37.66	$ 351.46	
Entrance rope & twinkle lighting, up lighting	1	$ 100.00	$ 100.00	$ 12.00	$ 112.00	
Arrival theme giveaways - Leis	1	$ 315.70	$ 315.70	$ 37.88	$ 353.58	
Buffet table linens, centrepieces, tea lights	1	$ 400.00	$ 400.00	$ 48.00	$ 448.00	
Dining table linens, centrepieces, tea lights	1	$ 300.00	$ 300.00	$ 36.00	$ 336.00	
Theme props, plants, incl delivery, install, teardown	1	$ 250.00	$ 250.00	$ 30.00	$ 280.00	
Volunteer costumes, including casino dealers, servers	1	$ 150.00	$ 150.00	$ 18.00	$ 168.00	
					$ 2,413.04	9%
FOOD & BEVERAGE (15%)						
All night buffets - incl passed trays, platters, fresh pizza, dessert Items	1	$2,200.00	$ 2,200.00	$264.00	$ 2,464.00	
Food for parent volunteers - based on 45 volunteers	1	$ 150.00	$ 150.00	$ 18.00	$ 168.00	
Beverages - including welcome mocktail, soft drinks, fruit juice, bottled water, coffee	1	$ 950.00	$ 950.00	$114.00	$ 1,064.00	
Popcorn machine - rental, delivery, install, pickup, supplies	1	$ 50.00	$ 50.00	$ 6.00	$ 56.00	
Hot dog machine - rental, delivery, install, pickup, supplies	1	$ 75.00	$ 75.00	$ 9.00	$ 84.00	
					$ 3,836.00	15%

cont'd...

http://safegradevent.com/tools/forms/eventbudget

EVENT BUDGET (cont'd) - NOVEMBER

AFTER-GRAD EVENT BUDGET (at date)						
ITEM DESCRIPTION	#	COST	SUB	HST	TOTAL	%
ENTERTAINMENT, GAMES, & CONTESTS (45 - 50%)						
DJ services, Karaoke services including all sound/tech	1	$1,000.00	$ 1,000.00	$120.00	$ 1,120.00	
"Live 2.30 - 4 am show" - Hypnotist	1	$2,000.00	$ 2,000.00	$240.00	$ 2,240.00	
Magician - 4 hour call	1	$ 500.00	$ 500.00	$ 60.00	$ 560.00	
Caricaturist - 4 hour call	1	$ 400.00	$ 400.00	$ 48.00	$ 448.00	
Caricaturist (2nd) - 4 hour call	1	$ 400.00	$ 400.00	$ 48.00	$ 448.00	
Airbrush Tattoo - 2 artists, 4 hour call	1	$ 500.00	$ 500.00	$ 60.00	$ 560.00	
Photo Booth - 5 hour call, delivery, install, tear down, all supplies, and attendant	1	$1,250.00	$ 1,250.00	$150.00	$ 1,400.00	
T-Shirt Table, incl shirts, pens for 200	1	$ 500.00	$ 500.00	$ 60.00	$ 560.00	
Photo loop screen rental	1	$ 25.00	$ 25.00	$ 3.00	$ 28.00	
Stand alone arcade games (Pinball Machine, Pac man)	1	$ 750.00	$ 750.00	$ 90.00	$ 840.00	
Pool table rental	1	$ 525.00	$ 525.00	$ 63.00	$ 588.00	
Foosball - Prize budget, becomes a prize after event use	1	$ -	$ -	$ -	$ -	
Air Hockey - Prize budget, becomes a prize after event use	1	$ -	$ -	$ -	$ -	
Audio Visual - TVs, DVDs, screens	1	$ 800.00	$ 800.00	$ 96.00	$ 896.00	
Video game systems - Prize budget, becomes a prize after event use	4	$ -	$ -	$ -	$ -	
PA sound system rental for bingo game/casino	1	$ 200.00	$ 200.00	$ 24.00	$ 224.00	
Bingo game - supplies only - donated	1		$ -	$ -	$ -	
Casino games rental -Blackjack, Wheel, Poker Tables	1	$1,250.00	$ 1,250.00	$150.00	$ 1,400.00	
Prize draw raffle drum - rental,dlvry, pickup	1	$ 20.00	$ 20.00	$ 2.40	$ 22.40	
Contest props and prizes	1	$ 150.00	$ 150.00	$ 18.00	$ 168.00	
					$11,502.40	44%
FUNDRAISING, PUBLICITY, PRIZES, MISC (5-10%)						
Event ticket printing	1	$ 50.00	$ 50.00	$ 6.00	$ 56.00	
Raffle ticket printing	1	$ 75.00	$ 75.00	$ 9.00	$ 84.00	
Faux casino dollars - printing charge	1	$ 25.00	$ 25.00	$ 3.00	$ 28.00	
Thank you ad in the local newspaper	1	$ 125.00	$ 125.00	$ 15.00	$ 140.00	
"just in case" money	1	$ 150.00	$ 150.00	$ 18.00	$ 168.00	
			$ -	$ -	$ -	
					$ 476.00	2%
Subtotal of Expenses :					$24,611.44	94%
Balance (projected Income minus projected expenses)					$ 1,638.56	

http://safegradevent.com/tools/forms/eventbudget

SUPPLIER QUESTIONS – NOVEMBER

SUPPLIER QUESTIONS

- Are you available on [date] the night of our event?
- What types of services or products do you provide?
- What is the cost of your service or product – there may be a catalogue or tariff list for all available products and services.
- How long have you been in business?
- Do you have event/liability insurance and can you provide a current certificate?
- Have you worked at/for a dry grad event before?
- How much space do you need, what size of footprint and any technical/power requirements?
- What is included with the service costs and what costs are additional? – consider delivery, installation; tear down, cleaning or repairs etc.
- How long do you need for teardown/pickup following the event?
- Can you provide "green" or "environment friendly" products?
- Will you be personally handling our event? If not, who will be our main contact person, what is their direct contact information, including a cell phone number?
- May we see a copy of your standard contract?
- What are your payment terms – do you require a deposit and if so, how much and when is it due? What is your cancellation policy?
- When would the balance owing be due? Is there a discount applicable if we pay by cash or cheque, rather than by credit card?
- Can you provide three references?

Try to provide the following event details to the supplier; it will assist them in quoting:

- The venue and specific location within the venue where that supplier/ product will be located.
- The group size (base this on the size of grad class and allow 10-15% extra for guests plus the number of anticipated volunteers – 15% of the total guest number)
- The call time, or the amount of time you will need the supplier/product to be onsite?

http://www.safegradevent.com/tools/forms/supplierquestions

FOOD PROVIDER QUESTIONS – NOVEMBER

FOOD PROVIDER QUESTIONS

- Do you have any particular style of food or menu items that you specialize in?
- What food items do you suggest for an overnight event and teen audience?
- Can you provide a "specialty themed" item to include in the menu?
- How do you address/handle dietary restrictions/food allergies? – consider vegetarian/vegan, kosher, gluten free. Can you provide special buffet signs?
- What costs are included in your contract and what costs are additional? – consider set-up, rentals, clean-up, staffing, overtime, service gratuities etc.
- Do/can you provide linens, glasses, serving pieces, silverware, tables & chairs, and decorations? Can you provide "green" or "environment friendly" products?
- What color & style of linens, glasses, plates, and accessories are available?– consider theme, ease of service -buffet style, service pieces – less silverware
- Will personally handle our event? If not, who will our main contact person be, and what is their direct contact information, including a cell phone number?
- How much time will you need for set-up and clean-up?
- Will you provide food for the suppliers/performers and volunteers that are onsite working the event and if so is there an extra charge?
- What would the cost-per-person be? (There may be set menu prices/per person pricing to choose from. Can we reduce costs by handling anything ourselves?
- Can extra non perishable food be packaged/taken to the school to reduce waste
- Can we see a copy of your standard contract?
- What are your payment terms – do you require a deposit and if so, how much and when is it due? What is your cancellation policy?
- When would the balance owing be due? Is there a discount applicable if we pay by cash or cheque, rather than by credit card?
- Can you provide three references?

Try to provide the following event details to the supplier; it will assist them in quoting:

- The event date/timing, venue and specific location within the venue where they/their products will be located.
- The group size (the size of grad class plus 10-15% extra for guests)
- The approximate number of onsite volunteers and suppliers (allow 25-30 for a group of 200, or 15% of the total guest number)

http://www.safegradevent.com/tools/forms/foodproviderquestions

PERFORMER QUESTIONS – NOVEMBER

PERFORMER QUESTIONS

- Are you available on (date) the night of our event?
- What types of performances/shows do you provide?
- How long have you been in business/performing?
- Do you have event/liability insurance and can you provide a current certificate?
- Is there a video/DVD we can view, or an upcoming performance we can attend?
- Have you ever worked at a dry grad event or for a teenage audience?
- What is the cost of your performance/show? Are there any additional costs associated with a late night performance?
- Do you supply everything, if not what do we need to provide?
- What are your technical requirements?
- How long do you need for teardown (important if there is another performance before/after this one)
- How much space do you need, what size of footprint?
- Do we need to provide food/refreshments and/or a green room? (a room for them to change, refresh, rest etc, a private space)
- Will you personally handle our event? If not, who would my main contact person be, and what is their direct contact information, including a cell phone number?
- May we see a copy of your standard contract?
- What are your payment terms – do you require a deposit and if so, how much and when is it due? What is your cancellation policy?
- When would the balance owing be due? Is there a discount applicable if we pay by cash or cheque, rather than by credit card?
- Can you provide three references?

Try to provide the following event details to the supplier; it will assist them in quoting:

- The event date/timing, venue, specific location within the venue where the performer will be located.
- The group size (base this on the size of grad class and allow 10-15% extra for guests, plus the number of anticipated volunteers – 15% of the total guest number)
- The call time/performance time (how long do you need the supplier to perform

http://www.safegradevent.com/tools/forms/performerquestions

PRIZE SOLICITATION LETTER – NOVEMBER

SCHOOL or GRAD LOGO

Date

Dear

As you are a member of the local business community, we would like to ask for your assistance in providing funds or a donation to be distributed as a "prize" to students from the school name graduating class of year. Every June, approximately 200 students graduate from school name.

Again this year, school name parents are hosting a school supported "safe, dry" (drug and alcohol-free) grad celebration on event date, immediately following the school sponsored formal ceremony and dinner/dance. The evening represents 6 hours of unforgettable activities and entertainment filled with dancing & karaoke, arcade & video games, interactive contests, temporary tattoos, magicians, caricaturists, a live performance by a hypnotist, and so much more. The night culminates in an exciting prize draw that sees every grad going home with a wonderful prize and some lifelong memories.

Our event relies on a great deal of volunteers and community support. While the event is partially funded by ticket sales, much of the money raised is through local businesses, right here, in our school community. Your support in helping us raise these funds goes a long way to providing some exciting prizes while at the same time, encouraging students to choose a safe, alcohol-free environment in which to celebrate their graduation. We hope that you will be interested in assisting us with a donation; any contribution is greatly appreciated. If you choose to support this initiative, we will be pleased to acknowledge your donation on our school name/grad/society website, in our parent newsletter, and in our local newspaper.

We encourage you to visit our website/page at website address to read more about our event and our efforts to keep our grads safe on graduation night. If you would like more information or have any questions, please contact me. And, we would be happy to make arrangements to pick up your donation at your convenience.

School name parents hope that the success of this all night safe, dry grad event will continue for years to come. We encourage you to be a part of this tradition that encourages a safe and healthy community and thank you in advance for your support. .

With our kindest regards,

Grad Chair name
School Name After-Grad Committee
Phone
Email

http://www.safegradevent.com/tools/forms/prizesolicitation

TUITION SOLICITATION LETTER – NOVEMBER

SCHOOL or GRAD LOGO

Date

Dear

As a prominent member of the local business community, we are writing to ask for your assistance in raising funds to distribute as tuition prizes for approximately 200 students from the school name graduating class of year. As you may be aware, tuition prices have been steadily increasing over the past few years. For example, a typical year at the local university name will now cost approximately $5,000 for tuition and fees and another $1000 for books. Most students will require some kind of assistance to complete a post secondary education whether at a university or elsewhere.

Again this year, school name parents are hosting a school supported "dry" (drug and alcohol-free) grad celebration on event date. At this all night event, we hope to give away three tuition prizes (each worth approximately $1500) to assist students in funding their post secondary education. Only those students attending the dry grad event will be eligible to win one of the tuition prizes. Your support in helping us raise these funds will assist students to finance their education, while encouraging them to choose a safe, alcohol-free environment in which to celebrate their graduation.

We hope that you will be interested in assisting these local students to achieve their goals by contributing $100 or more. School name will administer the tuition prizes; once a student enrolls in a post secondary institution (including universities, colleges, trade and vocational schools), the monies will be paid on the student's behalf.

We will acknowledge all tuition donations on our school name/grad/society website, in our parent newsletter and local newspaper. If you are willing to support our initiative, we are happy to arrange for pick up of your contribution (all cheques should be made payable to school district name). Please contact school name and phone number.

We encourage you to visit our website/page at website address to read more about our event and our efforts to keep our grads safe on graduation night. If you would like more information or have any questions, please contact me.

School name parents hope that the success of this all night safe, dry grad event will continue for years to come. We encourage you to participate in this tradition that encourages a safe and healthy community and we thank you in advance for your support. We look forward to hearing from you.

With our kindest regards,

Grad Chair name
School Name After-Grad Committee
Phone
Email

http://www.safegradevent.com/tools/forms/tuitionsolicitation

GRAD ATTENDANCE AGREEMENT – FEBRUARY

GRAD ATTENDANCE AGREEMENT
NAME OF SCHOOL PARENT SPONSORED AFTER-GRAD – date of event

The name of school year graduating class and their parents (the "Sponsors") will sponsor and plan an all night graduation celebration (AFTER-GRAD 2010) to be held immediately after the formal school sponsored Graduation Ceremonies and Dinner/Dinner Dance on June 10, 2010. While neither name of school, school staff nor school district (collectively the school) are sponsoring the AFTER-GRAD year, the sponsors, graduates, graduate's guests, and the school community wish to ensure a safe, responsible, and memorable celebration. Therefore, the parent organizing committee and sponsors requires each graduate to sign the following agreement as a condition of attendance.

Agreement of the Grad:
To ensure a safe, drug-free and alcohol-free all night After-Grad event at venue name beginning at date and time (immediately following the school sponsored dinner/dance) and ending at date and time, I agree to the following conditions of attendance:

- I understand and agree that the dinner/dance & After-Grad event have been combined on one ticket at one selling price, and are not offered as separate events to Grads
- This is a drug and alcohol free event (for all attending including those who may be of legal drinking age) and I agree to behave in a way that is conducive to a safe, drug-free and alcohol-free celebration. I will not consume, nor will I possess at any time, including on the buses, or at the event site (venue), any materials or items (drugs or alcohol) that may affect my behavior or that may be used to harm others, such as any items that could be considered to be or used as weapons.
- I understand and agree that the possession of or showing the effects of drugs, alcohol, or weapons will not be tolerated and will constitute grounds for dismissal from the event and that if I behave in a way that is deemed to be disruptive to the event, I will be detained by the onsite security personnel along with a parent volunteer, and my parents/guardians will be notified to pick me up immediately. Parents/guardians will be required to sign the student out of the event.
- Any additional transportation expenses incurred as a result of dismissal from the event will be my sole responsibility. Any prohibited substance or item found in my possession will be confiscated and I understand that a report will be filed with the local law enforcement agency, if applicable.
- I understand and agree that I am expected to remain at the event for its entirety (until time, date, and venue name) and that there are no in/out privileges. I understand and agree that name of school, and the parent sponsors along with the onsite parent volunteers are not responsible for me or any actions on my part, should I leave the event site (venue) prior to the conclusion of the After Grad event, (scheduled to conclude at time and date), with or without their knowledge or permission.. A dinner/dance only option will be available to guests, if requested. All attendants will be identified by an After-Grad wristband.
- I understand and agree that I will be transported by double decker bus from the venue name to the venue name. I also understand that I will be transported by bus from the venue name to the return location (pick up time and date) and that I am responsible for the arrangement of transportation home from the return location and that this transportation arrangement has been approved by my parents/guardians.
- I understand and agree that I will be searched upon entry and will not bring non-essential personal articles to the event. Should I have any of these items in my possession during the search at the time of event check-in, I will submit those items to the security personnel for safekeeping until the conclusion of the After-Grad. All items will be kept in a secure location, supervised by parent volunteers at all times.

My signature below indicates my complete understanding of and agreement with the terms and conditions set out above:
Name of Grad (please print clearly):_____Signature of Grad _____

If you plan to bring a guest to the After-Grad: Guest name (please print) _____
Guest's School/Workplace_____
Note: All guests must complete/sign a Guest Attendance Agreement Form, available at the office.

http://www.safegradevent.com/tools/forms/gradagreement

GRAD ATTENDANCE AGREEMENT (cont'd) – FEBRUARY

GRAD PARENT/GUARDIAN AGREEMENT
NAME OF SCHOOL PARENT SPONSORED AFTER-GRAD – date of event

The name of school year graduating class and their parents (the "Sponsors") will sponsor and plan an all night graduation celebration (AFTER-GRAD 2010) to be held immediately after the formal school sponsored Graduation Ceremonies and Dinner/Dinner Dance on June 10, 2010. While neither name of school, school staff nor school district (collectively the school) are sponsoring the AFTER-GRAD year, the sponsors, graduates, graduate's guests, and the school community wish to ensure a safe, responsible, and memorable celebration. Therefore, the parent organizing committee and sponsors requires each graduate to sign the following agreement as a condition of attendance.

Agreement of the Parent/Guardian of each Grad:
To ensure a safe, drug-free and alcohol-free all night After-Grad event at venue name beginning at date and time (immediately following the school sponsored dinner/dance) and ending at date and time, I agree to the following conditions of my graduating student's/guest attendance.

- I understand and agree that the After-Grad date celebration is <u>not a school sponsored event</u>, nor is it authorized or organized by the school, and forms no part of the formal graduating ceremonies, or requirements for attendance or graduation from name of school, whether or not any school staff attend, assist, or are invited to the name of school After-Grad year.
- My/our son/daughter, who is a member of the name of school graduating class of year, has my permission to attend the all night After-Grad event, taking place from time and date to time and date. I understand that the dinner/dance and the After-Grad event tickets are combined in one ticket at one selling price and are not being offered as separate events to grads. I understand and agree that grads who attend must remain until time and venue location ((a Dinner/Dance only option will be available for guests if requested). Students will be transported to the return location - arrival time is time and date and I have arranged transportation home for my/our child.
- I understand and agree to my/our son/daughter's requirement to abide by his or her agreement as set out above, and I agree to be available for contact at the telephone number listed below, and to attend at the site if the sponsors or the onsite After-Grad parent volunteers determine for any reason that I should be notified, or that my son/daughter should leave the site as a result of a breach of his or her agreement, or for any other reason.
- I understand and agree that written refund requests will only be considered and/or approved at the discretion of the sponsors, and only if an extreme situation prevents my child's attendance (student or family illness/injury).
- I agree to release and hold harmless the event sponsors/volunteers, name of school, venue name, and all agents, employees, and assignees of each for any damages suffered by me or my son/daughter arising from his/her attendance at this event.
- I am providing information regarding medical conditions/requirements, and food/drug allergies, and agree to this information being provided to onsite medical personnel if required (doctor, nurses, police)

My signature below indicates my complete understanding and agreement with the terms and conditions set out above; my son/daughter has signed the Attendance Agreement

Grad's Name (please print clearly	
Home Address	Home Phone
Name of Parent Guardian *(please print clearly)*	
Contact # during event*(event time)*	
Name of any person to whom grad may be released *(please print clearly, bring ID)*:	
Signature of Parent/Guardian	
List any/all medical conditions/requirements (any medication required and present during the event) and any food/drug allergies *(information is kept confidential)*	
T Shirt Size –please circle size	XS, S, M, L, XL, XXL, XXXL

http://www.safegradevent.com/tools/forms/gradagreement

GUEST ATTENDANCE AGREEMENT – FEBRUARY

GUEST ATTENDANCE AGREEMENT
NAME OF SCHOOL PARENT SPONSORED AFTER-GRAD - date of event

The name of school year graduating class and their parents (the "Sponsors") will sponsor and plan an all night graduation celebration (AFTER-GRAD 2010) to be held immediately after the formal school sponsored Graduation Ceremonies and Dinner/Dinner Dance on June 10, 2010. While neither name of school, school staff nor school district (collectively the school) are sponsoring the AFTER-GRAD year, the sponsors, graduates, graduate's guests, and the school community wish to ensure a safe, responsible, and memorable celebration. Therefore, the parent organizing committee and sponsors requires each guest of a graduate to sign the following agreement as a condition of attendance

<u>**Agreement of the Guest:**</u>
To ensure a safe, drug-free and alcohol-free all night After-Grad Event at venue name beginning at date and time (immediately following the school sponsored dinner/dance) and ending at date and time, I agree to the following conditions of attendance:

- I understand and agree that the dinner/dance & After-Grad event have been combined on one ticket at one selling price, and are not offered as separate events to Grads
- This is a drug and alcohol free event (for all attending including those who may be of legal drinking age) and I agree to behave in a way that is conducive to a safe, drug-free and alcohol-free celebration. I will not consume, nor will I possess at any time, including on the buses, or at the event site (venue), any materials or items (drugs or alcohol) that may affect my behavior or that may be used to harm others, such as any items that could be considered to be or used as weapons.
- I understand and agree that the possession of or showing the effects of drugs, alcohol, or weapons will not be tolerated and will constitute grounds for dismissal from the event and that if I behave in a way that is deemed to be disruptive to the event, I will be detained by the onsite security personnel along with a parent volunteer, and my parents/guardians will be notified to pick me up immediately. Parents/guardians will be required to sign the student out of the event.
- Any additional transportation expenses incurred as a result of dismissal from the event will be my sole responsibility. Any prohibited substance or item found in my possession will be confiscated and I understand that a report will be filed with the local law enforcement agency, if applicable.
- I understand and agree that I am expected to remain at the event for its entirety (until time, date, and venue name) and that there are no in/out privileges. I understand and agree that name of school, and the parent sponsors along with the onsite parent volunteers are not responsible for me or any actions on my part, should I leave the event site (venue) prior to the conclusion of the After-Grad event, (scheduled to conclude at time and date), with or without their knowledge or permission.. A dinner/dance only option will be available to guests, if requested. All attendants will be identified by an After-Grad wristband.
- I understand and agree that I will be transported by double decker bus from the venue name to the venue name. I also understand that I will be transported by bus from the venue name to the return location (pick up time and date) and that I am responsible for the arrangement of transportation home from the return location and that this transportation arrangement has been approved by my parents/guardians.
- I understand and agree that I will be searched upon entry and will not bring non-essential personal articles to the event. Should I have any of these items in my possession during the search at the time of event check-in, I will submit those items to the security personnel for safekeeping until the conclusion of the After-Grad. All items will be kept in a secure location, supervised by parent volunteers at all times.

My signature below indicates my complete understanding and agreement with the terms and conditions set out above:
Name of Guest (please print clearly) _____

Signature of Guest _____

Name of Grad (please print clearly) _____

http://www.safegradevent.com/tools/forms/guestagreement

GUEST ATTENDANCE AGREEMENT (cont'd) – FEBRUARY

GUEST PARENT/GUARDIAN AGREEMENT
NAME OF SCHOOL PARENT SPONSORED AFTER-GRAD – date of event

The name of school year graduating class and their parents (the "Sponsors") will sponsor and plan an all night graduation celebration (AFTER-GRAD 2010) to be held immediately after the formal school sponsored Graduation Ceremonies and Dinner/Dinner Dance on June 10, 2010. While neither name of school, school staff nor school district (collectively the school) are sponsoring the AFTER-GRAD year, the sponsors, graduates, graduate's guests, and the school community wish to ensure a safe, responsible, and memorable celebration. Therefore, the parent organizing committee and sponsors requires each guest of a graduate to sign the following agreement as a condition of attendance

Agreement of the Parent/Guardian of each Guest:
To ensure a safe, drug-free and alcohol-free all night After-Grad event at venue name beginning at date and time (immediately following the school sponsored dinner/dance) and ending at date and time, I agree to the following conditions of attendance:

- I understand and agree that the After-Grad date celebration is *not a school sponsored event*, nor is it authorized or organized by the school, and forms no part of the formal graduating ceremonies, or requirements for attendance or graduation from name of school, whether or not any school staff attend, assist, or are invited to the name of school After-Grad year.
- My/our son/daughter has my permission to attend the all night After-Grad event, taking place from time and date to time and date. I understand that the dinner/dance and the After-Grad event tickets are combined in one ticket at one selling price and that guests who attend the After-Grad must remain until time and venue location ((a Dinner/Dance only option will be available for guests if requested). Students will be transported to the return location - arrival time is time and date and I have arranged transportation home for my/our child.
- I understand and agree to my/our son/daughter's requirement to abide by his or her agreement as set out above, and I agree to be available for contact at the telephone number listed below, and to attend at the site if the sponsors or the onsite After-Grad parent volunteers determine for any reason that I should be notified, or that my son/daughter should leave the site as a result of a breach of his or her agreement, or for any other reason.
- I understand and agree that written refund requests will only be considered and/or approved at the discretion of the sponsors, and only if an extreme situation prevents my child's attendance (student or family illness/injury).
- I agree to release and hold harmless the event sponsors/volunteers, name of school, venue name, and all agents, employees, and assignees of each for any damages suffered by me or my son/daughter arising from his/her attendance at this event.
- I am providing information regarding medical conditions/requirements, and food/drug allergies, and agree to this information being provided to onsite medical personnel if required (doctor, nurses, police)

My signature below indicates my complete understanding and agreement with the terms and conditions set out above: my son/daughter has signed the Guest Attendance Agreement

Grad's Name (please print clearly
Guest's Name (please print clearly)
Home Address
Home Phone
Name of Guest's Parent/Guardian
Contact # during event *(event time)*
Name of any person to whom grad may be released (please print clearly, bring ID):
Signature of Guest's Parent/Guardian
List any/all medical conditions/requirements (any medication required and present during the event) and any food/drug allergies *(information is kept confidential)*
T Shirt Size –please circle size   XS   S   M   L   XL   XXL   XXXL

http://www.safegradevent.com/tools/forms/guestagreement

EVENT SCHEDULE – MARCH

SCHOOL OR GRAD LOGO

AFTER-GRAD EVENT SCHEDULE

EVENT DATE

AFTERGRAD TEAM

NAME	ROLE	ONSITE CELL NUMBER
	Venue Manager	
	Venue Contact onsite	
COORDINATORS		
	Overall Event Coordinator	
	Volunteer Coordinator	
LEAD VOLUNTEERS		
	Entertainment Handler	
	Wellness Room – Doctor	
	Wellness Room – Nurse	
	Wellness Room – Nurse	
	Wellness Room – First Responder/Paramedic	
	Police Officer – on duty	
	Oversee Lounge/Games Room	
	Oversee Nightclub	
	Oversee Main Concourse	
	Oversee Casino (Pit Boss)	
	Oversee Prize Draw	

http://www.safegradevent.com/tools/forms/eventschedule

EVENT SCHEDULE (cont'd) – MARCH

EVENT FLOW /TIMING

TIMING	RESP	DESCRIPTION
10.00 am	Venue	Access for loading in – all rooms except main concourse
	Name	Provide Master Attendance list to venue
	Suppliers	All suppliers delivering between 12 noon and 5 pm today – see Install Schedule
	Parents	Additional deliveries, see Install Schedule
9.00 pm	Volunteers	All volunteers, except wellness team- touch base meeting
	•	Review roles and responsibilities
9.30 pm	SUB	Access for loading in – main concourse
	•	All teams/volunteers set up their areas
	•	Dealers, dress in costumers, practice dealing
Install of Outside Entrance treatment		
	Names	Follow instructions on table marked "Outdoor Entrance"
Outside Clothing Tables		
	Names	All clothing assembled in alpha order by last name
Main Concourse Set up		
	Names	Install Hot Dog Machine – set up condiments table
	Names	Install Popcorn Machine - set up condiments table
	Names	Tattoo Area – supplier will handle this
	Names	Caricaturist Tables – set up chair, lamp
	Names	Set up Video Games - DDR, Rock Band
	Names	Set up T-Shirt tables, shirts, lists, pens ready to go
	Names	Set up Coat Check, tables
	Names	Set up Buffet table – see instructions on set up table
	Names	Washrooms – put out some of the 'refresh amenities'
Lounge	Names	Set up Video Games - XBOX and Nintendo Wii
		Karaoke – DJ will take care of this
		Arcade Games – already in place by supplier
		Foosball, Air Hockey in place with all parts, ready to play
		Photo Booth – already set up, with attendant in place
	Names	Digital Photo Loop – set up
	Names	Buffet table linens, grass skirting, fish nets & seashells
Nightclub	Names	Set up buffet items – see instructions on set up table
	Names	There will be tiki torch centerpieces coming from the dinner/dance to go on the tables, scattered along with new candles, which will need to be lit
	Names	Glow necklaces, bracelets and beach balls (these need to be blown up) can be stored under the buffet until needed.

http://www.safegradevent.com/tools/forms/eventschedule

EVENT SCHEDULE (cont'd) – MARCH

Casino		Names	Set up Bingo game, player supplies, check microphone
		Names	Set up Registration table, "Panther" bucks (casino money), red dealer pens, Master attendance list copy for sign out
Wellness Room			
		Names	Set up mats, linens, & pin "allergy alert" list to board
	10.00 pm	Names	Check all buffets, ensure all items are available
	10.15 pm	Names	In place at the dinner/dance to move the guests on buses take the novelty items, the ID wristbands, the name lists, the driver gratuities and the bus escort scripts

---

DINNER/DANCE VENUE

10.30 pm	Names	Pick up dinner/dance items that are being shared with the After-Grad event, from the dinner/dance venue – see list
10.30 pm	Names	In place to get ready for guest transfer • all toys placed on seats, alternating, boy/girl on the buses • brief and distribute driver gratuities • lists and ID bracelets set up inside with 45 of each colour
10.40 pm	Names	Begin distributing wristbands and loading the buses – load half the group on this first shuttle and the other half on the second shuttle split the group evenly between both buses • Buses will take at least 10 minutes to load, so grads may not arrive until approx 10.55 pm • Bus escorts – please get on the microphone once the bus starts moving to read your script

---

AFTER-GRAD VENUE

10.30 pm	Names	**Main concourse** - Start up Hog Dog Machine
	Names	**Main concourse** - Start up Popcorn Machine
	Names	**Entrance** - performers begin to arrive - please greet & show them their location and then make sure they are in position, ready to go, have what they need
	Names	**Entrance** - In place to assist with security firm
10.45 pm	Names	In position outside and inside, ready to receive guests Someone needs to light the tea lights (Nightclub) – thanks
	DJ	**Entrance** - Music playing outside front entrance
10.50 pm	Guests	**Entrance** – First guests arrive, coaches return for second shuttle with bus escorts
	Names	**Outside Clothing** – In position ready to receive guests
	Names	**Coat Check** – In position ready to receive guests

http://www.safegradevent.com/tools/forms/eventschedule

EVENT SCHEDULE (cont'd) – MARCH

	Names	**Pirate/Mermaid** In place outside, ready to receive guests, handing out leis. Pirate handing out gold doubloons
	Names	**Photographers** - In position to take photos for the digital loop – try to get some guests arriving with their novelties
	Names	**Servers** - Ready with "mocktails" & canapés - some pouring, some serving, some taking empty glasses, some serving food – veggies/dip
	Names	**Wellness Room** - Set up to receive as needed – mats/blankets in place, all meds to go to the doctor onsite from the security & coat check
	Names	**Casino** – In position at registration to sign in guests, hand out "Panther" bucks (casino money)
	Names	**Bingo** – Dealers & Bingo callers can spell each other off, or help each other with this one when there are guests
	Names	**Pool Table** – Oversee play
	Names	**Nightclub** - In place with glow sticks at the entrance and please keep a watchful eye on the back doors at all times
	Names	**T-Shirts** – One pen to every other grad/guest – extra or leftover shirts go to the coat check once this table closes
11.30 pm	Names	**Contests** – all contests are now up and running
	Names	**Washrooms** – first check of washrooms – then every 30 minutes from now until 5 am – refresh with amenities as needed
11.45 pm	Names	**Outside** - Once the last guest has passed through the doors, any unclaimed clothing moves to the coat Check- it goes through security before it enters the building
	Names	**Outside** Teardown – the outside decorating and lighting gets torn down - everything goes back into the set up area for pick up tomorrow by suppliers
12 am	Names	**Casino** - Costumed servers begin serving water, food etc.
1 am	Venue	delivery of volunteer food to the wellness room
1.30 am	Names	**Nightclub/Prizes** - all prizes need to be moved into the nightclub in preparation for the Prize Draw – someone needs to keep these secure during the band and hypnotist's performance – thanks
2.00 am	Band	Live performance – 30 minute play time

http://www.safegradevent.com/tools/forms/eventschedule

EVENT SCHEDULE (cont'd) – MARCH

2.30 am	Band		Released, the band may watch the hypnotist because they cannot tear down yet – provide payment - remind the band that their equipment must be removed by noon on Friday – there is another event in this space
	Names		**Nightclub** - 24 chairs now onstage for hypnotist - ask him how they are to be arranged (stored behind the stage curtain)
2.30 am	Hypnotist		Onstage now, 1.5 hour show – DJ will introduce himself
3.00 am	Karaoke		Released now, will tear down now as this room is closing down – no payment at this time
	Caricaturists		Released now, provide payment
	Magician		Released now, provide payment
		Photobooth	Released now, provide payment
		Tattoo Artists	Released now, provide payment
3.30 pm	Names		**Lounge** - close the lounge, clean up, move decorating items back to the set up area for supplier pickup tomorrow.
	Names		**Casino** – close the casino, clean up, move decorating items back to set up area for supplier pick up tomorrow. – the Pit boss & registration volunteers to determine a casino winner and a bingo winner – for the prize draw
3.45 am	Names		Please go around announcing the prize draw to all guests starting at 4 am – they have to be in that room in order to win
3.50 am	Names		**Nightclub** – Prize volunteers can now make their way to the nightclub to help with the prize draw - 2 people to record all the winners (this is a gaming requirement; please record names carefully/accurately).
4.00 am	Hypnotist		Released, provide payment
4.05 am	Names		**Prize Draw** - Announce that the prize draw is about to take place - grads should get water/food, take a washroom break, before we start – they have to be in the room to win.
			Keep the prizes moving along in order on the table, someone to hand them to the prize MC, someone to add another to the table as we move along, and record the exact winning names of the tuition/bursary winners.
	DJ		Play the 'grad' song just before Prize Draw begins
4.30 am	Bus Escorts		Gather up extra granola bars and bottled water, to load on to the buses when they arrive, along with recycling and garbage bags.
	Names		**Coat Check** – In place, ready for the grads/guests to come running as soon as the prize draw ends

http://www.safegradevent.com/tools/forms/eventschedule

EVENT SCHEDULE (cont'd) – MARCH

4.45 am	Buses	Spot the buses, provide cash gratuities, and put coloured signs in bus windows
	Names	**Bus Escorts** -Be ready to stand by your bus – you should have your food and bags onboard • Check all wristbands, grads/guests must board the bus that matches their wristband because our lists must match the names of those onboard, in case of an accident enroute • Put your coat or purse on the seat behind the bus driver, to reserve that seat – you need to sit up front, and be near the microphone if needed.
4.50/5 am	Names	**Nightclub** - Announce that buses are now loading, and the procedure re: coloured wristbands.
	Names	**Line Control** - please direct guests to the bus that has the same colour sign as their wristband – release 8-10 at a time to maintain control and keep the flow going.
5.00 am	DJ	DJ is released to tear down, provide payment
	Names	**All rooms** - teardown begins in every room - everything goes back to the set up area except the larger pieces in the casino and arcade games in the Lounge **We only have until 6 am to get it all cleaned up**
5.30 am	Buses	Buses arrive to return location, RCMP are onsite
6 am	Names	One last walk through the venue to ensure that we have not forgotten anything or missed cleaning anywhere

---

Friday Morning
10 am – 2 pm   Supplier pick up for all rentals, band equipment etc. See Install/teardown schedule

THANK YOU VOLUNTEERS – YOU MADE IT HAPPEN!

http://www.safegradevent.com/tools/forms/eventschedule

VOLUNTEER GRID – MARCH

VOLUNTEER GRID (positions are based on a group of 200)																		
		9 - 9.30	9.30 - 10	10 - 10.30	10.30 - 11	11 - 11.30	11.30 - 12	12 - 12.30	12.30 - 1	1 - 1.30	1.30 -2	2 - 2.30	2.30 - 3	3 - 3.30	3.30 - 4	4 - 4.30	4.30 - 5	5 - 5.30	5.30 -6
All Volunteers		Meet																	
Outside setup/tear	8																		
Inside decor setup	10																		
Tech games setup	1																		
Bus Transfer to Event	4																		
ID Wristbands	2																		
Clothing Distribution	10																		
Registration/ Security Check	4 to 8																		
Mocktail Servers	6																		
Outside Teardown	8																		
Coat Check	12																		
T-Shirt Table	4																		
Wellness Team	4																		
Casino Dealers + Pit Boss	13																		
Casino Greeters	2																		
Casino Servers	2																		
Entertainment Handler	1																		
Nightclub	4																		
Floaters	8																		
Concession /Vendors	4 to 8																		
Games Room Supervisor	1																		
Games & Contests	6 to 10																		
Digital photos	2																		
Prize Draw	5																		
Line Control	2																		
Bus Sign Out	4																		
Bus Escorts	10																		
Teardown	4 to 8																		

http://www.safegradevent.com/tools/forms/volunteergrid

VOLUNTEER GRID (cont'd) - MARCH

VOLUNTEER GRID (positions are based on a group of 200)	
VOLUNTEER POSITIONS - DESCRIPTORS	
Outside Entrance Setup//Teardown	Includes set up and tear down all of entrance decorations, clothing tables - carpet, stanchions, lighting, theme props, organizing clothing - Lead + 7 parents set up & tear down
Inside Decorations Setup	Lead + 12 volunteers set up various rooms including all indoor decorations, large scale props, buffet tables, dining tables, and novelty items (beach balls, glow sticks etc.)
Tech Games Setup	Includes set up any of the electronic games including Nintendo Wii, XBOX 360, DDR, Rockband, TVs, Digital loop
Double Decker Transfer to Event	2 Male, 2 Female volunteers place novelty items on the seats of each bus, ride the shuttle, must be comfortable speaking on the mic with a prewritten script. Two shuttles total for each couple.
ID Wristbands	Volunteers sign out grads/guests from the Dinner/Dance, put on ID wristbands for Double Decker transfer
Clothing Distribution	Organize clothing in alpha order for Grad/guest arrival - to be taken through security check. All unclaimed bags must be cleared by security and then kept in the coat check
Registration/ Security Check	Volunteers process entry, and/or assist onsite security firm
Mocktail Servers	Costumed servers pour/serve tropical mocktails & canapés on arrival
Coat Check	Lead + 11 volunteers receive all clothing, purses, storage bags from security check, organize all alpha & distribute when grads/guests leave at 5 am
T-Shirt Table	Lead + 3 volunteer set up shirt display, distribute shirts using guest attendance list for sizing.
Medical Staff - Doctor, Nurses, Police Officer	Doctor remains in the Wellness Room at all times, Nurses can take shifts, Police Officer roams the event
Casino Dealers	Pit Boss +13 volunteers run Casino games including 8 - blackjack, 1 wheel, 2 poker tables, Bingo, 1 Pool Table
Casino Registration	Manage Sign in list, distribute "casino money", retain chits for departing/returning grads
Casino Servers	Costumed servers serve food and beverages to players
Entertainment Handler	Volunteer ensures that all entertainers/performers/onsite suppliers have what they need for setup, provide food & beverages and assist in managing line-ups
Nightclub	Lead + 3 volunteers provide supervision, hand out glow sticks, beach balls, keep rear doors secure, manage buffet, distribute bottled water, and set up 24 chairs prior to hypnotist performance.
Floaters	Assist as needed, washroom checks every 30 minutes, ensure that no one is ill or isolated. Use discretion and refers needed to Wellness room personnel
Concession/ Vendors	Cooking, serving, clean up as required
Lounge Supervisor	Lead provides supervision, manages buffet, ensures distribution of bottled water
Games & Contests	Volunteers oversee games/inflatables, run contests, record names for prize draw
Digital photographers	Volunteers roam the event, take digital pictures (own cameras) download them every 30 minutes.

cont'd

http://www.safegradevent.com/tools/forms/volunteergrid

VOLUNTEER GRID (cont'd) – MARCH

VOLUNTEER GRID (positions are based on a group of 200)	
Prizes	Assist with distribution of prizes, prize table set up, recording "winners" list
Line Control - Checkout	Assist with the line up, prepare buses for boarding, distribute extra food on the buses, load extra garbage and recycling bags, ensure guests have all of their personal belongings including medications
Bus Sign Out	Manage alpha lists, direct grads/guests to buses, and escort as needed
Bus Escorts - Male & Female per	1 male/female bus escort to ensure safety, assist with ill passengers, distribute bottled water, granola bars
Teardown/Cleanup	Additional cleanup, pack up and store decor items, props etc.
Installation Volunteer	Handle all daytime supplier installations on event day - preferably a non Grad parent
Additional Jobs:	Pick up popcorn machine and mats for wellness room from the school
	Buy popcorn supplies, including oil, kernels, shaker flavours, small bags
	Purchase bottled water and deliver to the venue on the day of the event
	Return bottles from the event to the School for recycling
	Return costumes to the Costume Shop

http://www.safegradevent.com/tools/forms/volunteergrid

INSTALLATION SCHEDULE – MARCH

NAME OF SCHOOL, DATE OF EVENT, VENUE NAME
AFTER- GRAD INSTALLATION SCHEDULE

Company /Supplier	Description	Location	Install Time	Details	Contact Name	Office Phone	Onsite Cell #
Band	Band equipment (drum kit, instruments)	Nightclub Stage	Anytime after 12 noon	drum kit to sit on carpet for easy removal prior to hypnotist performance			
Decor Rental Company	Décor & Linens (see quote sheet for full list)	Set up Area	Between 10 am and 12 noon	invoice after event			
Outdoor Rental Company	Blue Carpet, Stanchions (see quote for full list)	Set up Area	Between 10 am and 12 noon	carpet and ropes must be blue Invoice following event			
Island Photo booth	Photo booth	Lounge/Games Room	After 12 pm, traveling all day to location	payment upon installation			
Marquee Sign	Flashing Welcome Sign	Main Concourse Outside, West Corner	After 2 pm - in use until then	set up outside entrance Donation - no payment required			
Casino Rentals	Casino Games (blackjack tables, poker tables, wheel)	Casino	Between 10 am and 12 noon	see floor plan for placement			
Table Linen Company	Linens etc (see quote sheet for full list)	Set up Area	After 3 pm, before 5 pm	venue storage Invoice following event			
Billiards Company	Pool Table	Casino	Between 10 am and 12 noon	see floor plan for placement details			
AV Company	AV -TVs, Lights	Set up Area	Between 10 am and 12 noon				
Volunteer Parents	Change of Clothing Bags	Set up Area	Various throughout day	all in venue storage			

http://www.safegradevent.com/tools/forms/installschedule

FLOOR PLAN – APRIL

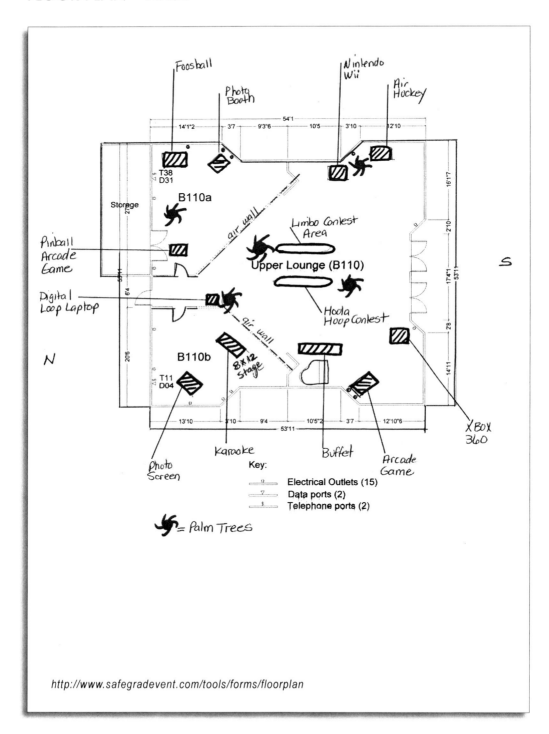

http://www.safegradevent.com/tools/forms/floorplan

MASTER ATTENDANCE LIST – MAY

NAME OF SCHOOL, DATE OF EVENT, VENUE NAME
AFTER-GRAD MASTER ATTENDANCE

	LAST	FIRST	GROUP
1	Adams	Mary	Grad or Grad Guest
2	Barker	Joe	Grad or Grad Guest
3	Coleman	Veronica	Wellness Team - Police Officer
4	Corn	Sonya	Grad or Grad Guest
5	James	Thomas	School Admin - Principal
6	Jensen	Lori	Volunteer
7	Longman	Eric	Wellness Team - Nurse
8	Maker	Jasmine	School Admin - Ed Assist for Grad - Joe Barker
9	Marshall	Berry	Grad or Grad Guest
10	Masters	Steve	School Admin - Vice Principal
11	McConnell	Alex	Volunteer
12	Piers	Mary	Volunteer
13	Sidney	Rick	Volunteer
14	Steadman	Patricia	Wellness Team - Doctor
15	Stevens	Ian	Volunteer
16	Sutton	Jane	Supplier/Entertainer
17	Sutton	Steve	Supplier/Entertainer
18	Thompson	Susan	Volunteer
19	Thompson	Merv	Volunteer
20	Waterling	Brian	Volunteer
21	Waterling	Carey	Volunteer

http://www.safegradevent.com/tools/forms/masterattendance

MASTER GUEST LIST – MAY

	Grad Last Name	Grad First Name	MED Alert	T-Shirt Size	T-Shirt Picked up	Guest Last	Guest First	MED Alert	T-Shirt Size	T-Shirt Picked up	EXIT Alert	NOTES
						NAME OF SCHOOL, DATE OF EVENT, VENUE NAME AFTER- GRAD MASTER GUEST						
1	Adams	Mary	X			Smith	John					
2	Barker	Joe				Carling	Carol	x			x	
3	Corn	Sonya				n/a	n/a					
4	Marshall	Berry	X			Johnson	Sylvia				x	
5												
6												
7												
8												
9												
10												
11												
12												
13												
14												
15												
16												
17												
18												
19												
20												
21												
22												
23												
24												
25												
26												
27												
28												

http://www.safegradevent.com/tools/forms/masterguest

SUPPLIER AGREEMENT - MAY

NAME OF SCHOOL, DATE OF EVENT, VENUE NAME
AFTER-GRAD SUPPLIER AGREEMENT

Please review this agreement and advise of any incorrect or missing information

Supplier:	Contact Name				
Office Tel:	Local Office Number	Email:		Cell:	
AG Contact - Prior to Event:		Email:	Phone:	Cell:	
AG Contact - During Event:		Email:	Phone:	Cell:	
Venue Contact – During Event:			Office:	Cell:	

EVENT OVERVIEW:
The After-Grad is a **parent operated,** school supported event, designed to provide our grads with a **safe, drug and alcohol free** event. Grads will be transferred to/from the event by mode of transfer and they will remain at the event from event timing. All grads/guests will be identified by wristbands.

EVENT DETAILS:

Event Date:	Date of the event
Event Time:	Timing of the event – may use the Event Flow timing here
Number of Guests:	Total number of guests (grads/guests only, not volunteers)
Venue:	Venue name
Supplier Location:	Location within the venue, i.e. nightclub, main concourse, games room
Directions & Parking:	
Load In/Access:	Details on how the supplier can access the venue and in particular the location (for example, the nightclub may have a loading dock/bay)
Tear Down/Strike:	Timing and instructions regarding the tear down of equipment, pickups for rentals etc

PRODUCT/ SERVICE DETAILS:

Product/Service:	List what is included in the supplier/rental contract, including delivery, set up, cleaning, onsite assistance etc.
Cost:	List all costs associated with the contract including labour, delivery, installation, parking, taxes, etc.
Payment:	How & when payment will be made – by cheque, credit card, onsite or following the event etc.

ADDITIONAL NOTES and QUESTIONS:
- Please forward an invoice immediately if you require payment on event day
- Please forward a copy of your insurance certificate by email or fax

http://www.safegradevent.com/tools/forms/supplieragreement

FOOD & BEVERAGE ORDER – MAY

| \multicolumn{9}{c}{AFTER- GRAD F and B ORDER} |

Supplier	#	Unit Cost	Sub Total	Service Gratuity	Sub Total	GST ONLY	Total	Notes
Based on projected # of Guests:	200							
Food & Beverage - All Night Long								
Upon Arrival - Passed Trays								
Crudités & dip, leftovers on buffets	4	$ 20.00	$ 80.00	$ 12.00	$ 92.00	$ 4.60	$ 96.60	Served by volunteers
Tortilla Chips & Salsa, leftovers the buffets	6	$ 12.00	$ 72.00	$ 10.80	$ 82.80	$ 4.14	$ 86.94	Served by volunteers
"Pink Panther" Mocktail - by the Punch Bowl	6	$ 44.00	$ 264.00	$ 39.60	$ 303.60	$ 15.18	$ 318.78	
Main								
40 pizzas	40	$ 15.95	$ 638.00	$ 95.70	$ 733.70	$ 36.69	$ 770.39	
Fresh Fruit Platters	4	$ 75.00	$ 300.00	$ 45.00	$ 345.00	$ 17.25	$ 362.25	one per buffet
Deli Platter	4	$ 95.00	$ 380.00	$ 57.00	$ 437.00	$ 21.85	$ 458.85	one per buffet
Dessert								
160 Small Cookies	160	$ 0.75	$ 120.00	$ 18.00	$ 138.00	$ 6.90	$ 144.90	40 per buffet
Granola Bars	100	$ 1.00	$ 100.00	$ 15.00	$ 115.00	$ 5.75	$ 120.75	25 per buffet
							$ 2,359.46	
Volunteer/Supplier Food								
Deli Platter	1	$ 95.00	$ 95.00	$ 14.25	$ 109.25	$ 5.46	$ 114.71	from 1 am
Sandwich Tray - 15	15	$ 3.95	$ 59.25	$ 8.89	$ 68.14	$ 3.41	$ 71.54	from 1 am
							$ 186.26	
Beverages								
Bottled Water	400	0	$ -	$ -	$ -	$ -	$ -	Supplier donation
Soft Drinks	300	1.25	$ 375.00	$ 56.25	$ 431.25	$ 21.56	$ 452.81	all 4 buffets
Fruit Juice	100	1.75	$ 175.00	$ 26.25	$ 201.25	$ 10.06	$ 211.31	all 4 buffets
Fresh Coffee x pot	10	10	$ 100.00	$ 15.00	$ 115.00	$ 5.75	$ 120.75	from 1 am
							$ 784.88	
Pricing is an example only and does reflect accurate venue pricing								
Taxes may differ from province to province, and year to year								

http://www.safegradevent.com/tools/forms/fandborder

PERFORMER AGREEMENT – MAY

NAME OF SCHOOL, DATE OF EVENT, VENUE NAME
AFTER-GRAD PERFORMER AGREEMENT

Please review this agreement and advise of any incorrect or missing information

Supplier:	Contact Name		
Office Tel:	Local Office Number	Email:	Cell:
AG Contact - Prior to Event:		Email: Phone:	Cell:
AG Contact - During Event:		Email: Phone:	Cell:
Venue Contact – During Event		Office:	Cell:

EVENT OVERVIEW:
The After-Grad is a **parent operated,** school supported event, designed to provide our grads with a **safe, drug and alcohol free** event. Grads will be transferred to/from the event by mode of transfer and they will remain at the event from event timing. All grads/guests will be identified by wristbands.

EVENT DETAILS:
Event Date:	Date of the event
Event Time:	Timing of the event – may use the Event Flow timing here
Number of Guests:	Total number of guests
Venue:	Venue Name
Supplier Location:	Location within the venue, i.e. nightclub, main concourse, games room
Directions & Parking:	
Load In/Access:	Details on how the performer can access the venue and in particular the location, for example, the nightclub may have a loading dock/bay
Tear Down/Strike:	Timing and instructions regarding the tear down of equipment, pickups for rentals etc

PRODUCT/ SERVICE DETAILS:
Talent/performance:	List what is included in the performance contract, including call time, breaks schedule, type of performance and inclusions
Tech Requirements:	List tech requirements here or refer to the "rider" you have in hand
Dress Code:	Expectations as well as "theme" dress requests
Green Room:	List where he/she can change, refresh, practice etc.
Cost:	List all costs associated with performance including travel, parking, expenses, taxes etc.
Payment:	How & when payment will be made – by cheque, credit card, onsite or following the event etc.

ADDITIONAL NOTES and QUESTIONS:
- Please forward an invoice immediately if you require payment on event day
- Please forward a copy of your Insurance Certificate by email or fax

http://www.safegradevent.com/tools/forms/performeragreement

BUS ESCORT SCRIPT – JUNE

BUS ESCORT SCRIPT

Good Evening Ladies and Gentlemen and welcome aboard your express bus to New York City!

Tonight we invite you to spend a little time enjoying the sounds and sights of the "City that doesn't sleep" You are in for a great night in the Big Apple!

Your visit to New York City includes a stop at Central Parkland where you can sing a little Karaoke, play a little XBOX or Wii, enjoy a game of Pinball, compete at Air Hockey or Foosball, or just sit back and relax. And don't forget to step into the Photo Booth to take that all important photo of you and your friends, a memory for life!

Or maybe you would like to take a stroll down Broadway Avenue, where you just might meet a Magician, finally get that Tattoo you've been wanting, or have your portrait drawn by a Caricature Artist. Along the way, you can enjoy a fresh Hot Dog or slice of Hot Pizza, pick up your souvenir T-Shirt, play a little DDR, or how about some Rock Band?

Then it's off to the 1920's Casino to try your luck. We've got blackjack, poker tables, a wheel and Billiards. Take a load off, sit awhile and listen to some cool jazz, play some Bingo, or you can even catch a 'silent' flick - one of your favourites is playing on the big screen, and the popcorn is ready!

Then, if you still have time and some energy left over, take a wander over to Studio 54, the hottest nightclub in New York City. Dance the night away to your favourite tunes, and then stick around for a live performance by "MESMER" the hypnotist.

And then just when you think you can't have another minute of fun, you can join your entire Grad class for Parkland's huge Prize Draw with over $ 10,000 in prizes and gift certificates including some fantastic electronics -all to be won by you, the 2008 Parkland Grad Class.

Don't forget, our photographer is in town to snap your favourite memory, so be sure to have your picture taken while you are here. Enjoy the After-Grad, class of 2008 – this is your PARTY!

http://www.safegradevent.com/tools/forms/busscript

BUDGET ANALYSIS – JUNE

NAME OF SCHOOL, DATE OF EVENT, VENUE NAME AFTER- GRAD BUDGET ANALYSIS					
Payee	Description	NET	GST/HST	TOTAL	Notes
Big Bus Company	Transportation to venue	$ 600.00	$ 72.00	$ 672.00	invoice forthcoming
Perfect Printing Inc.	Event Tickets	$ 40.00	$ 4.80	$ 44.80	
Tattoos are Us	Temporary Tattoo Artists	$ 500.00	$ 60.00	$ 560.00	pd onsite
Vegas Casino Games	Casino Games	$ 1,250.00	$ 150.00	$ 1,400.00	due following event
Subtotal: Budget Costs		**$ 2,390.00**	**$ 286.80**	**$ 2,676.80**	
Budget Reconciliation					
Carryover		$ -			
Ticket Sales Income		$ 18,000.00			
PAC Donation		$ 1,500.00			
Local Town Council Grant		$ 1,250.00			
Fundraising - Bottle Drive Campaign		$ 1,800.00			
Fundraising - Grocery Cards Campaign		$ 1,500.00			
Private Donations		$ 2,200.00			
Total Income from All Sources		$ 26,250.00			
Total Expenses including GST		$ 2,676.80			
Balance - Credit or Debit		**$ 23,573.20**			

http://www.safegradevent.com/tools/forms/budgetanalysis

Linda Hunter

Linda Hunter has over 20 years of conference and event planning experience, and has successfully produced five unforgettable After-Grad events for Parkland Secondary School, including the founding event in 2006.

Linda lives in Sidney, British Columbia where she shares her heart and her home with her husband, 3 grown children and her mother, and where she remains open to possibility and dedicated to service.

Her hope for all high school graduates is that they will embrace a safe dry After-Grad event so that their graduation really can be the time of their life and not the end of their lifetime.